KATHERINE PATERSON

A Stubborn Sweetness

and Other Stories for the

Christmas Season

WESTMINSTER
JOHN KNOX PRESS
LOUISVILLE · KENTUCKY

"Angels and Other Strangers," "Guests," "Broken Windows," and "Woodrow Kennington Works Practically a Miracle" appeared in *Angels and Other Strangers: Family Christmas Stories* published by Thomas Y. Crowell in 1979 and reprinted here by permission of HarperCollins Publishers. "Exultate Jubilate," "Star Lady," "In the Desert, a Highway," "Merit Badges," "Watchman, Tell Us of the Night," "My Name Is Joseph," "No Room in the Inn," "The Handmaid of the Lord," and "A Stubborn Sweetness" were originally part of a collection titled: *A Midnight Clear: Family Christmas Stories*, published by Lodestar Books in 1995. "On the Night of His Birth: Mary's Story" was published as "Mary" in the *Presbyterian Survey* (now called *Presbyterians Today*), December 1985, and is reprinted by permission of Presbyterians Today.

First edition
Published by Westminster John Knox Press
Louisville, Kentucky

13 14 15 16 17 18 19 20 21 22—10 9 8 7 6 5 4 3 2 1

Book design by Erika Lundbom
Cover design by MTWdesign.net

Library of Congress Cataloging-in-Publication Data

Paterson, Katherine.
  [Short stories. Selections]
  A stubborn sweetness and other stories for the Christmas season / by Katherine Paterson. —1st edition.
    pages cm
  All but one story previously published in the anthologies "Angels and Other Strangers" and "A Midnight Clear."
  ISBN 978-0-664-23915-2 (alk. paper)
  1. Christmas stories, American. 2. Children's stories, American. [1. Christmas—Fiction. 2. Short stories.] I. Paterson, Katherine. Angels and other strangers. II. Paterson, Katherine. Midnight clear. III. Title.
  PZ7.P273St 2013
  [Fic]—dc23

                                                          2012048002

PRINTED IN THE UNITED STATES OF AMERICA

♾ The paper used in this publication meets the minimum requirements of the American National Standard for Information Sciences—Permanence of Paper for Printed Library Materials, ANSI Z39.48-1992.

Westminster John Knox Press advocates the responsible use of our natural resources. The text paper of this book is made from 30% post-consumer waste.

Most Westminster John Knox Press books are available at special quantity discounts when purchased in bulk by corporations, organizations, and special-interest groups. For more information, please e-mail SpecialSales@wjkbooks.com.

A Stubborn Sweetness

and Other Stories for the

Christmas Season

For Carl, Gina, Isaac, Ella, Levi,
and
all the members of the family that is
First Presbyterian Church of Barre, Vermont,
with love and gratitude

Contents

Acknowledgments

Most of the stories in this book were read aloud by my husband, the Rev. Dr. John Paterson, at Christmas Eve services in three different parishes—Takoma Park Presbyterian Church, Takoma Park, Maryland; Lafayette Presbyterian Church, Norfolk, Virginia; and First Presbyterian Church, Barre, Vermont. The stories were written over a period of more than forty years, and all but one of them have been previously published. "Angels and Other Strangers," "Guests," "Broken Windows," and "Woodrow Kennington Works Practically a Miracle" appeared in *Angels and Other Strangers: Family Christmas Stories* published by Thomas Y. Crowell in 1979 and reprinted here by permission of HarperCollins Publishers. "Exultate Jubilate," "Star Lady," "In the Desert, a Highway," "Merit Badges," "Watchman, Tell Us of the Night," "My Name Is Joseph,"

"No Room in the Inn," "The Handmaid of the Lord," and "A Stubborn Sweetness" were originally part of a collection titled *A Midnight Clear: Family Christmas Stories*, published by Lodestar Books in 1995. A slightly different version of "Star Lady" was included in the Christmas Eve issue of the Norfolk-based *Virginian-Pilot* in 1982, and "Exultate Jubilate," in an abridged version, appeared in *Good Housekeeping* in December 1995. "On the Night of His Birth: Mary's Story" was published as "Mary" in the *Presbyterian Survey* in December 1985. "Why the Chimes Almost Rang" is making its debut in this volume.

I am grateful not only to my husband for reading my stories aloud from the pulpit but to the congregations who listened to them and have remained such a treasured part of my life over the years.

Nearly every year since the first stories were published someone has asked for permission to read or tell one or another of these stories. And although I like being acknowledged as the author, you do not have to ask for special permission to tell or read the stories. Permission is granted. I am honored if you want to use any of them as part of your Advent or Christmas celebration. In the case of reprinting, whether in electronic or printed form, you will need to get permission from the publisher.

Exultate Jubilate

C hristmas is over. Sally is putting the children to bed, and I am sitting in the living room staring at a rocking horse and trying to figure out what happened to me last night. You must understand, first of all, that I have always entertained a certain sympathy for Scrooge. There he was, going about his business as best he knew how while all around him the world was going mad. 'Tis the season to be jolly? Come, now. What is there to be jolly or merry or even mildly happy about? How can anyone who watches the evening news on a daily basis work up a case of holiday cheer? Frankly, I weary of Christmas carols that start jangling through the malls at Halloween. The decorations on the lampposts that the city fathers drag out every Friday after Thanksgiving have begun to show their age. And so have I.

My wife is another story. She goes into a frenzy of decorating and baking and, since August, has been in a panic trying to decide whether or not to give a present to the Steadmans. I just try to stay out of her way.

I want my kids to be happy, but it's hard to be patient when they pester me for months for junk they've seen on TV that anyone over ten knows wouldn't last out the twelve days of Christmas. Can someone explain to me why, as the days grow shorter, the pitch of children's voices gets higher and higher? Besides, this year business has been, if not bad, certainly not robust, and I simply didn't have the money, not to mention energy and goodwill, to waste on the latest fad.

Still, the only reason I didn't go around literally grunting "Bah! Humbug!" this year was because of the kids. They are only three and six, and I am enough of a hypocrite not to try to ruin their excitement, much as my head aches to tone down the shrill. But somehow I drew the line at going to the Christmas Eve service last night. Once I slid out from under my mother's "Thou shalt nots," I became quite happily an Easter, Christmas, and whenever-my-mother-was-visiting Christian. But this year even Christmas seemed too much.

I told my wife I would stay behind to organize the stocking gifts and put the rocking horse together. Every year it's two or three in the morning before we can get to bed. And then we're too angry with each other to sleep. The year of Mike's tricycle was a low point in Christmases past—one reason Jenny was getting a rocking horse.

"The children will be so disappointed if you don't come," she said.

"Oh, they don't really expect me to go to church."

"But it's snowing, and you know how I hate to drive in the snow."

"Why is it that I have three more years of payments on a certain four-wheel-drive Subaru wagon?"

"But I don't like leaving you here all by yourself on Christmas Eve," she said. "You'll get gloomy and moody."

"In two hours," I whispered, lest any little ears be nearby, "I'll have that rocking horse put together, and all we'll have to do is stuff the stockings and dream of sugarplums." That cinched it. She remembered all too well the long night of the tricycle.

"Daddy isn't feeling up to church tonight," she told the children. I coughed obligingly and helped her zipper the snowsuits and yank on the boots, and happily waved them off to church.

A half-hour later, I was not so happy. The rocking horse that I had so carefully purchased was proving to be, in my mother's picturesque phrase, "an instrument of the devil."

It was not on rockers, but attached to its stand by huge, coiled springs. I had, by the hardest effort, pulled three of the four springs and hooked them into the stand. But every time I got the fourth nearly in place—sweating and straining to make it stretch to the last eye—the spring would recoil viciously, gouging my flesh as it flew through my hand.

I was glumly staring into the living room fireplace with a large brandy in my hand when the doorbell rang. My impulse was to ignore it. Sally had the garage opener. She wouldn't be ringing the front doorbell, and nobody we knew would be dropping in for a visit. The bell rang twice before I roused myself, put down my drink, and shuffled to the door.

Through the peephole I could see a youngish looking man. He was wearing a windbreaker, but his head and hands were bare. He was carrying a pasteboard box and he looked frozen.

I opened the door about an inch. "Yes?"

He smiled. His lips were cracked and his nose and cheeks raw. "Would you like to buy some Christmas greens?"

The man had obviously not seen the inside of our house. "Sorry," I said, starting to close the door on his smile.

"Well, merry Christmas to you," he was saying when I remembered the stupid horse. Maybe the guy could help.

I opened the door wide. "Come in," I said with heartiness so false any fool would have suspected me of being up to no good. "Come in and get warm, at least. You must be frozen."

He put down his box of greens, stamped the snow off his thin shoes, and stepped in gratefully. "Not many sales tonight," he said. "I expect most people are all ready for Christmas."

"Yeah," I said. "Could I get you something hot? I think there's still some coffee."

"Gee," he said. "That's real nice of you." He followed me down the greenery-festooned hall to the kitchen. "Wow," he said, "you sure don't need more greens. You're loaded."

"My wife's a little bit crazy on the subject of Christmas," I said, pouring out a mug of coffee for each of us. "Milk and sugar?"

"If it's no trouble." He held the mug out for me to put in the milk and then the sugar, and then stick in a spoon. "Thank you," he said, stirring deliberately while he looked around our big kitchen. Sally had wreaths and ribbons even in there. His hands were so chapped they looked as though they'd been bleeding.

"Smells like Christmas," he said.

I hadn't noticed, but in addition to the evergreens the room was full of the warm odor of cinnamon and cloves and the Christmas bread that Sally had baked that afternoon.

"Nice, isn't it?" he said.

"Well, yes, I suppose so. If you like that sort of thing." My mind was on getting the horse done before Sally and the children got back, but I couldn't very well snatch the coffee I'd just given him from his hands.

"I guess you have a pretty tree, too."

Well, what could I do? He obviously wanted to see our tree. I led him back down the hall to the living room. Our house is not one of these energy-efficient moderns. It's Victorian with a fifteen-foot ceiling, and the tree scraped it. I think Sally picked out the house so she could have monster Christmas trees. There is certainly no other reason for a ceiling of that height. You should see our heating bill.

The visitor was standing there, his mouth open, his eyes shining like a three-year-old's. "That's the most beautiful tree I ever saw in my life," he whispered. "Yes, well," I felt almost apologetic. "My wife—"

He turned, his face still full of awe. "She must be a wonderful person."

"As wives go . . ." I tried to joke, but it wasn't going to work. The guy was as sincere as a cocker spaniel. "Don't let your coffee get cold," I said.

He ducked his head and took a sip, but over the rim he was eyeing my sound system. Oh, dear. Maybe he was casing the joint. I took his elbow to steer him to the family room, where one three-legged rocking horse sat waiting, but he resisted me.

"I know I shouldn't ask you . . ." He smiled his childlike smile. It was impossible to believe that such a lovely smile, cracked lips and all, belonged to a potential thief. "I mean, you've been so nice, but I'm so hungry for real music. Just while I'm drinking your good coffee?"

He looked hungry for meat and potatoes, but how could I refuse such a request? "Okay," I said, "a bargain. You can choose any music in the cabinet if you'll help me put together a rocking horse for my daughter."

His smile broke into a laugh. "I'm getting the best end of that." He handed me his still almost-full cup and fairly ran to the cabinet.

While he fingered the CD's and tapes lovingly, I wondered what he might choose. There wasn't much there that would appeal to a person of his class. There were dozens of recordings of Christmas carols—even one, so help me, of those cartoon chipmunks singing traditional tunes.

"Here," he said, his eyes glowing. "This one, please."

"Are you sure?" He was handing me Mozart. The Colin Davis London Symphony recording of Mozart's sacred music. Now wouldn't you have been surprised?

"Do you mind?" he asked anxiously when he saw my hesitation.

"No, of course not," I said.

"I don't look like a Mozart lover, right?" His smile was on crooked now.

"Well, I mean . . ." There was no way of getting out of that one. I put down the coffee cups and inserted the tape.

I waited for the great "Kyrie in D Minor" to boom out, and after adjusting the sound slightly, picked up the coffee cups and started for the family room and the horse.

"No!" He grabbed my wrist. Coffee sloshed into the saucers from both cups. "Listen."

"Kyrie Eleison! the voices demanded. *Lord have mercy!* "Christe Eleison!" *Christ have mercy!* I thought I had heard it before, but I realized, as I looked at my visitor, that I had never really heard it. His eyes were closed. I felt distinctly uncomfortable. "Come on," I said, slipping my wrist out from under his hand, being careful to keep from spilling coffee on Sally's rug. "We've got to get that fool horse done before my family gets home."

He opened his eyes and looked at me. I thought he was going to object, but he grinned. "Yes," he said, "our bargain."

"It's in there, too." I jerked my head at the sound system. "The music goes all over the house."

"Oh," he breathed. "That's wonderful. You can live in music." He followed me to the den.

There sat, or should I say, sagged the horse with Mozart showering down upon its head. "If you pull that spring," I said nodding at it with my head, "I'll try to yank this side in toward you so you can hook it."

He was listening to the Kyrie and not to me. I hated to interrupt him, but we did have this bargain. "The horse," I said with a bit more urgency in my voice.

"They're likely to get home any minute . . ."

He nodded, but I knew he wasn't paying attention to me. I should have been angry, but somehow, he was forcing me to listen to the music, too. I handed him back his coffee. "Just through the Kyrie, all right?" I said. "Then we do the horse." I'm not sure if he heard, but he took the coffee and sat cross-legged on the floor, his head cocked toward the wall-mounted speaker.

I sat on the couch, watching him listen, but it was not a stranger's profile I was seeing but the face of my father singing this very Mozart one Christmastime when the civic chorus had decided against the usual *Messiah*. My father died when I was seventeen, so I must have been a young teenager.

I loved to watch my father sing. Of all the faces in the chorus, his was the one that appeared to be listening rather than showing off. He always seemed to believe the music that he sang. And although I was an arrogant kid full of questions and resisting any answers, I loved the humble reverence I saw in him. I never told him though. It wouldn't have been cool or neat or whatever our catchphrase was in those days. And then he died.

I went to the kitchen and cut a piece of Sally's Christmas bread and brought it to the stranger—to make up for never having told my father that I loved to watch him sing. "You're too kind," the young man murmured. Me, too kind? Lord have mercy, indeed.

How, I wondered, in some future Christmas would my children remember me? Certainly not as I remembered my father—his face glowing with the glory of the music he sang.

I could almost see a huge festive table with a grown-up Mike and Jenny and their families gathered around. And Sally, white-haired and wrinkled, but still not a bad-looking woman. "I wish your father could be here today," she was saying.

"Dad?" Mike was frowning. "He'd hate it. I mean, the very fact that we are here would mean that civilization hadn't blown itself to bits. You know how he hated to be proved wrong about anything."

"Mike! What a thing to say!" Thatta girl, Sally.

"You remember the news bulletins?" Mike went on.

"Children,"—now Jenny, my sweet little girl, has jumped into it—"children, the minute the tree went up your grandfather would begin reading aloud items from the newspaper to prove how awful the world was—that there was no peace, no goodwill, no hope, no joy—"

"Exultate Jubilate!" the choir sang out. With a chill of relief, I shook off the ghost of Christmas-yet-to-come and turned my attention again to my visitor. His face shone as his cracked lips moved, mouthing the Latin words of joy and exultation. How could he, with raw face and chapped and bleeding hands, be joyful? How, in fact, could the starving Mozart have known such a moment of exquisite joy? How could a baby born in a barn bring such beauty, such glory into this greedy, self-destructive, cruel world?

Suddenly I heard the clatter of the garage door. I jumped from the couch.

"They're back!"

"Oh." The young man hastily picked the crumbs of bread off his windbreaker and jeans and popped them into his mouth. He half rose. "I'm sorry," he said. "I was lost . . ."

"It's too late. I'll get them into the front room. You just slip out when you can, and make sure the door is shut." He looked puzzled, maybe a little hurt. "The horse," I explained. "I don't want the children to see it." And I slammed the family room door on his confused and embarrassed face.

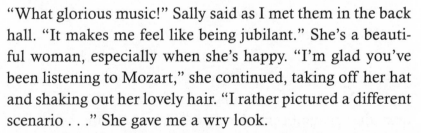

"What glorious music!" Sally said as I met them in the back hall. "It makes me feel like being jubilant." She's a beautiful woman, especially when she's happy. "I'm glad you've been listening to Mozart," she continued, taking off her hat and shaking out her lovely hair. "I rather pictured a different scenario . . ." She gave me a wry look.

"Okay," I said to the children. "Let's take all the boots and snowsuits off in the back hall."

"It's cold out here, Daddy," Mike started. "I wanted to take them off in the family room."

"Now, now," I said, "no complaints. Joy to the world, and all that!"

"'Cause it's Christmas!" Jenny shrilled, but her voice didn't pierce through me as it had earlier.

"That's right," I said and bent down to help with her boots but kissed her cheek instead.

"You tickle!" She giggled and put her fat little arms around my neck. I bent closer to the boots so she wouldn't see my eyes. I was feeling very rich.

We had our family time together before the living room fire. I never heard the stranger leave, but then it must have been sometime after the "Alleluia." I can't imagine he would have left before that heavenly "Alleluia."

"This has been a lovely evening." Sally sighed as she tied the ribbon on the last package. "The nicest Christmas Eve I can remember."

"Yes," I said. "Thanks to you. Everything looks so beautiful and smells so good."

She laughed. "It's the same every year. I didn't think you noticed—except for the bills."

"Well, I noticed, and I like it."

"It was your music that did it for me," she said. "I wouldn't have thought of Mozart for Christmas Eve, but it's perfect. You have no idea how it felt to open the door and hear that magnificent 'Exultate' come pouring out." She smiled. "What a wonderful idea."

Then I remembered the horse and the stranger I'd left in the family room. "Oh, Sally," I said, rushing down the hall. "I totally forgot . . ."

I opened the door. He was gone. I think I was relieved. I'm sure I wouldn't have known how to explain him.

Sally was behind me. "You did it," she exclaimed. "Good work."

Then I realized that the horse was no longer sagging but stood upright, proudly stretched on all four legs—ready to gallop its way into Christmas morning. The stranger had kept his side of the bargain.

So here I sit trying to figure it all out. Who would believe that a man who is still closer kin to Scrooge than to Tiny Tim would, on a bleak midwinter night, be visited by an angel?

I think I'll go put on the Mozart.

Star Lady

On the first morning of her retirement, Rosamund
McCormick got up at a quarter to seven. There was so
much to do. She would begin with the house.

The real estate agent had warned her that December
was a terrible month to sell a house. Even in a good year,
people didn't buy in the winter, he had said. But Rosamund
hadn't gotten to be one of the state's "Outstanding Women
of Business" by listening to other people whine. There
were plenty of wealthy young couples on the lookout for
a beautifully kept ninety-year-old house with hand-carved
mantelpieces and hardwood floors.

The neighborhood was no longer a handicap, she told
herself over coffee. There had been a time when her son
had urged her to move. Many of the older houses had
deteriorated, and nearly everyone she knew had fled to

the suburbs. The patrons at Miller's grocery store had changed first in color and then in language, and, sad to say, there was usually a wino or two hanging about the small parking lot.

Grace Church, in which Rosamund had been baptized and married, had changed, too. When dear Dr. Lancaster died, they called a bearded boy right out of seminary who spoke to God as though He were a fraternity brother. The educational building, named the Weatherford-McCormick Building for her husband and her father, was turned into a day care center. And the choir—she shuddered. The choir loft that had once resounded with Bach oratorios now yipped with discordant modern jingles. She blanched to recall one awful one in which the refrain had been "Hooray for Jesus! He's our man!" Rosamund refused to make a fuss. She quietly moved her membership to the large downtown First Church, where the choir all had trained voices and the Trinity was addressed with proper deference.

During those years when the neighborhood as well as the church and the corner grocery were going downhill, Rosamund had held on to her house. She had lived in it all her life, and she was simply too busy to take on the task of moving. Her husband, who had come into the family department store business when they married, died three years after her father, so Rosamund had to take over.

Now the neighborhood was on the verge of becoming fashionable once more. It was the perfect time to sell—a good time to leave. She had nothing to keep her. The business was in capable hands, her son was dead. She paused to refill her cup. Gail had remarried, of course, in less than two years. And, as if Rosamund hadn't suffered enough, the children, James's children, her grandchildren, had been adopted by Gail's new husband. She hardly saw them anymore.

She had planned to begin with the attic and work down through the house, throwing away everything except the antiques. She felt a great need to strip away all the physical encumbrances of her life and start afresh. But in the attic there were old letters and pictures, a worn-out football jersey, a weight-lifting set. No, it was not a day for the attic. Besides, from the window she could tell it was going to be one of those wonderful, almost spring like December days. She would begin with the garden. Hard physical exercise was the thing she needed.

The only time Rosamund ever allowed herself to wear trousers was in the garden. She used an old pair that had been her husband's, adding one of his hunting shirts for warmth. She tied her hair up in a scarf and put on her sturdy gardening shoes and yellow gloves.

She was pruning a rose bush when she spied the child staring at her through the hedge. Since she was on her knees, they were almost at eye level, except that it wasn't his eyes that she noticed first but the red, very runny nose. The hedge—she must make a note to call the nursery on Monday—was a bit scraggly at that spot, and the boy was standing in the alley behind it, obviously watching her.

"May I ask what you want?"

"Hi," he said, almost at the same moment.

"What are you doing here?" She couldn't help feeling that he had invaded her privacy, if not her territory, as he elbowed his way through the hedge.

"Watch that hedge!"

"Don't worry. It don't scratch much."

"I didn't think it would hurt *you*." But the boy, who

seemed to be about eight, wasn't listening. He was taking her measure with his eyes, looking at her yellow gloves, her oversized pants, her worn shirt, even the threadbare canvas pad on which she was kneeling.

"Ain't got no coat, I bet," he said sympathetically.

"Of course I have a coat. I'm just not wearing it at the moment."

He nodded, a smile lighting up his dirt-smeared features. "Sure, lady," he said. "I understand."

"Understand? Understand what?"

"It's tough, being winter and all. But I want you to know you got friends in this world."

Rosamund was too startled to reply. Where had this creature come from? As if in answer, he nodded south. "They explained everything to us in Sunday school. People need to know that God loves them and that they got friends in the world."

"Well, that's very nice. Thank you very much," said Rosamund in her briskest voice, the one that sent the most persistent sales representatives backing out of a room. The boy didn't notice. "Well, good-bye," she said loudly, rising and pulling off her scarf. She would try to finish the roses at a better time.

"White hair," the boy said. "You really are old. Wow."

"I am sixty-five," Rosamund said tightly. "Not dead yet."

"Sixty-five." His eyes, a sort of grayish blue, widened. "My grandma is only fifty. You're old enough to be my great-grandma."

"Hardly. Don't you have a tissue or something for that nose?"

"No'm." He snuffled noisily.

For an awful moment she thought he was going to wipe

his nose with his hand. She turned away. "Well, good-bye," she said and began to hurry toward the back steps. He came trotting after.

"We're supposed to come in and give you Christmas cheer."

"Thank you just the same. I'm quite cheerful enough already."

He snuffled once more. "But," he said, "if I don't pay you a visit, I don't get a star. See, the team that gets the most stars . . ."

What idiotic nonsense! Still what could you expect from a church that sang "Hooray for Jesus?"

"Oh, all right." She was trapped and she knew it. "Come on in—for a minute. I'm busy."

He followed so closely up the back stairs that she was afraid he would trip on the heels of her shoes, but somehow they made it to the porch. "Wipe your feet on the mat, please," she said, demonstrating. He nodded vigorously, elaborately smearing the garden mud from one end of the mat to the other, losing a bit on the porch in his enthusiasm.

At the door, she slipped out of her garden shoes and was walking stocking-footed over to the kitchen closet when she realized he had taken off his sneakers and was tiptoeing after her in gray socks that she imagined she could smell across the room. Never mind. She'd feed him and dispense with him in ten minutes flat.

"I suppose you'll want something to eat," she said as she put on her house shoes and stowed the garden shoes in the closet.

"Oh, no," he said piously. "It's against the rules to take people's food."

"And I suppose it's also against the rules to blow your nose?"

"I don't think so," he said. "Preacher didn't mention nothing about it." The back of the hand headed toward the nose.

"Wait," she said, diving into her purse, which lay on the kitchen counter. "I may have a tissue." But she came up with a handkerchief of Belgian linen and lace that she had bought on her world tour two years before. It couldn't be helped. She handed the handkerchief to the boy.

He took it without thanks and blew his nose loudly and wiped it with all the ceremony he had expended on the doormat minutes before. Then he held it out to her.

"No, no," she said. "You keep it. You might need it later."

He nodded and stuffed it into his jeans pocket.

"Well—" How was she to get rid of him? "Thank you for your visit."

But he was just then settling himself on the kitchen stool. "I guess you're all alone in the world. Got no one to spend Christmas with or anything."

She opened her mouth, but before she could protest, he went on. "No kids. Not even a job, I bet."

"If you don't mind . . ."

"My mom's got a job. She puts the little ones in the center. Works out real good."

"That's nice," Rosamund said tightly.

"Yeah. I didn't know how lucky we were." He smiled sweetly at her. "I was just this grabby little kid, thinking about what I was going to get for Christmas. Stuff like that."

"I see. Well, it's been nice visiting with you, uh—"

"Buddy," he said. "Name's Buddy."

She might have guessed. "Thank you, Buddy. Now. I'm very busy. I'm going to be moving soon and I have a lot to do."

"Moving? They gonna make you move?"

"Buddy, really, I must—"

"But miz—miz—that's terrible."

"Not your worry." She wasn't about to give the child her name or any more of her time. She swept him out the door, handing him his sneakers on the porch. He didn't seem offended and called out cheery greetings as he went, reminding her more than once that God loved her and that she was no longer friendless. She smiled back primly, but the minute he was gone, she collapsed against the door, laughing until the tears rolled down her cheeks. She had to go poking about in her handbag for a tissue, which made her start laughing all over again.

She made a conscious effort to pull herself together. She was not going to become one of those old women who talk to themselves or laugh out loud in empty houses. But at the moment she couldn't think of anyone to call and tell. Her friends wouldn't be able to imagine how very comical it was—that solemn little runny-nosed boy bringing her Christmas cheer so his Sunday school team could get a star. And she had given him her Belgian linen handkerchief . . . James would have loved it. But James was dead and she hardly ever saw his wife or children anymore.

The laughter evaporated at the thought of her grandchildren, who were growing up without her. She had tried to visit, but Gail and she had never been close, and Gail's new husband seemed ill at ease in her presence. James's children, who had once been so tiny and dear, had suddenly become loud and unmannerly, eager to be off to some party or other. She had begun spending all her holidays in Florida. It was easier on everyone.

A few days later, there was a note on her door when she

got back from the hairdresser's. It was on lined notebook
paper and clumsily decorated with crayoned stars and
Christmas trees.

> **Dear   fiend** (she could barely decipher the
> handwriting),
>
> this is to invite you to our Christmas Joy
> Service on Christmas Eve at 7 p.m. at Grace
> Church. We want you to know that God
> loves you and you got lots of friends.
> There will be eats, too.
>
> Your special friend, Buddy Collins
>
> P.S. Don't worry. You can wear your old
> clothes. It don't matter.

Christmas at Grace Church. She remembered all too well
the last Christmas Eve service she had attended in Grace
Church. There were at least eight different-colored electric
flames in the windows. The minister paraded two dozen
or more squawky-voiced children to the front to sing some
jangly tune . . . with rhythm instruments. Rosamund sighed.
Tacky. That was the only word for it.

She allowed herself, just for a moment, to go back to the
Christmas Eves years ago when the sanctuary had been dimly
lit with a pair of standing candelabra among the poinsettias.
Into the darkness and the hush, the choir, sounding like
a single voice from the vestibule, began the ancient carol
"Let all mortal flesh keep silence . . ." Then they walked in
solemn procession down the main aisle, carrying candles,
the haunting melody growing in power as they came, until
at last they massed under the majestic pipes of the choir loft

ablaze with light. The music soared, filling the church and reverberating from the great dark beams of the rafters:

"Alleluia, Alleluia, Alleluia, Lord most High!"

She shivered at the memory of it. The wonder and the power and the mystery. And now . . .

She balled up the grubby little note and dropped it into the hall basket. But Buddy, as she found, was not to be dismissed so easily. Two days before Christmas, she was in the midst of decorating her tree when the doorbell rang.

"Hi," he said cheerfully.

"Oh, Buddy, I'm very busy right now. I'm decorating my Christmas tree."

"You got a tree?" He rushed by her at the door to come in for a look. "Oh." He sounded relieved. "It's real tiny." He went closer to the table on which the tree stood. "Not even real." This time his voice segued into its sorrowful key. "But it's nice." He looked up, his dirty little face radiating sincerity.

"Thank you, Buddy."

"It's real nice you keep trying. Some old people just give up."

"Do they, now?"

"Yeah. You ought to see the ones over at the home. It's real pitiful—some of 'um don't even know who they are anymore."

"You'll be glad to know that I still know who I am."

"Good for you." He beamed, patting her arm. "You just keep it up." He picked up a glass ball from the box on the table and shook it.

"Buddy," she said as quietly as possible, "that ornament is nearly one hundred years old. Would you be kind enough to put that back into the box? Very carefully."

"Huh? Oh, sure." She watched him, hardly breathing, as his hand, which was too big for his small body, lurched against the side of the box, rattling the delicately painted glass ball back into its place.

"Cost too much to get new ones these days, don't it?"

"Yes," she said, sighing with relief. "Well, Buddy, it was nice of you to come, but I am busy right now."

"I could help decorate your tree."

"No!" The word came out more sharply than she'd intended. "It's just that I'm getting ready to move and . . ."

"Oh, yeah." Sympathy poured through the dirt on his face. "Oh, yeah. I almost forgot." He started backing toward the front door. "But don't you worry. Just remember—God loves you, and you got friends in this world."

"I won't forget, Buddy. Be sure your team gets another star."

He missed the irony, of course, beaming his most evangelical smile. That's who he reminded her of. Those television evangelists with their toothy smiles. Only their faces were cleaner.

She forgot about her little gospel bearer until the phone call early Christmas Eve morning.

"Rosamund? Merry Christmas! It's me, Gail."

"Yes, Gail." She could feel her body stiffening.

"It's been too long since we've seen you."

"Yes, well, I've been quite busy."

"We'd love to have you join us for dinner tomorrow."

"I have plans."

"I would have called you earlier, but I just assumed you'd be in Florida as usual."

"No. I'm moving down as soon as I sell the house. I felt the need to stay and get it ready."

Why was Gail laughing? Rosamund hadn't said anything funny. She'd never understood Gail. She felt the impulse to slam down the receiver but restrained herself. "Thank you for calling," she said crisply.

"No, no, no, wait—" Gail was trying to suppress her giggles. "I have to explain."

"Yes?" She was curious despite her annoyance.

"Peter called." Gail could only mean Peter Freedman, the new president of Weatherford Department Store, Inc. "Someone called the office to ask about you."

"About me?"

"Yes, apparently"—and here another giggle bubbled up—"apparently there is a rumor going around the neighborhood that you have lost all your money and are on the verge of eviction."

"Eviction?"

"I know it's crazy, but that's what the minister told Peter."

"What minister?" But she knew the answer. "That bearded boy at Grace Church?"

"That's the one."

"Buddy." Rosamund bit the name as though it were a profanity. "Pardon?"

"I've got something I have to attend to, Gail. I'll talk to you later."

"About dinner . . ."

"Later." She clanged down the phone. That dirty-faced, runny-nosed busybody, making a fool of her at the church, at the company, even with Gail. Just because she'd tried to be nice.

She had a cup of tea to calm herself before calling the church office.

"Grace Church. God loves you, and you have friends in the world. Merry Christmas!"

"Yes. This is Rosamund Weatherford McCormick. I would like to speak to the pastor."

"He's not in right now. Can I take a message?"

She was delighted to note that all the bounce had seeped out of the secretary's voice. "In that case," she continued, carving each word out of ice, "I would like the telephone number of a child by the name of Buddy Collins. I understand he attends your Sunday school."

"Uh, Mrs. McCormick. Maybe you ought to speak to Bill first."

"Bill?"

"Reverend Farley."

"I thought you just said he wasn't in."

"He's not, but—"

"Then I will take the Collins's number."

"I think Reverend Farley wants to talk to you about a misunderstanding."

"The telephone number, if you please."

"I don't know if they have a phone. I don't seem to have a listing . . ."

She finally extracted the street address from the reluctant secretary. It was one of the tumbledown houses that backed hers on the alley. She went to her bedroom, carefully applied her makeup, and dressed in a soft wool peacock-blue dress, and—although it was totally inappropriate for morning wear—pinned a large diamond brooch at her throat. Then she put on her cashmere overcoat. If Buddy had difficulty identifying quality, his mother ought to be able to recognize that Buddy's Sunday school project was not teetering over the edge of either senility or poverty.

She stormed down the alley, around the corner, and up the street, looking for the proper number. She guessed the house before she got to it—one of the once handsome Victorian mansions that had been chopped into apartments. The grassless front yard was overrun with small children and dogs, all of which seemed to be wagging their tongues at her. In a tangle of frantic barks and high-pitched squeals—"Whatcha want, lady? Whatcha want?"—she made her way through the yard to the front door. There was no bell, so she knocked loudly, nearly bruising her knuckles in the effort to make herself heard over the din.

At last someone came to the door. Buddy, carrying a baby almost as large and runny-nosed as himself.

"Oh." He cocked his head. "My mom's at work." And then suddenly, as though finally recognizing her above the cashmere collar and taking in the meaning of her visit, he hung his head. "Preacher told me you ain't being thrown outta your house."

"No," she said, her anger already evaporated.

"I ain't going to bother you no more. Don't worry." He began to close the door with his foot, juggling the baby as he did so.

Just then a little girl who had been in the yard bumped past her and shoved the door wide open. "This your star lady, Buddy? The one you was telling about?"

"Shut up!"

"Is it? Is it?" She danced around, looking at Rosamund from every possible angle.

"No!" Buddy yelled. "You don't get no stars for bothering rich people. You just get stars for helping the poor and needy."

"You didn't get a star for me?" Rosamund asked.

"I got the wrong house," he said. "Supposed to see this old lady on welfare, and I got the wrong house. Preacher give me the devil for it, too."

Rosamund smiled despite herself. "We're going to get your star back," she said.

The boy sneaked a look and when he saw the smile, he smiled shyly back, shifting the squirming baby to his other hip.

"I don't care," he said. "It was dumb, anyway."

"But the preacher ought to know."

"Know what?" He snuffled.

"That . . . sometimes . . . rich old ladies need friends, too."

"Yeah?" He jiggled the baby to quiet it, his eyes on its almost hairless head.

"Wanna come to church with me tonight?" he whispered.

"Of course," she said.

The sanctuary was lit with the same garish electric candles, and the music, if anything, was worse than she had remembered. The congregation was a variegated mix of race and age.

In a specially designated front section, all the children in Buddy's Sunday school class were sitting with their star people. The children's beaming faces alternated with the tired faces of the neighborhood's aged outcasts. Rosamund was sure that the man two down from her was one of Miller's grocery store's winos, his breath coming down the pew sour and strong. One the other side of Buddy, a little girl, pink ribbons bouncing in her black plaits, was proudly arranging the crutches of her star lady under the pew in front.

Instead of the stately alleluias of bygone years, Rosamund could hear the cry of a sleepy baby in the rear, echoed by the hacking cough of an old man at the end of her row.

After an exuberant attack on "Hark! The Herald Angels Sing" that would have roused the dead to protest, the bearded young preacher read the Christmas story in a jarring modern version. "What is the message of Christmas?" he asked. "What does it mean to us that this baby was born in a barn all those years ago? Today, in Grace Church, when we hear this story, what does it make us want to say to our neighbors?"

"God loves you!" the children yelled. "And you got friends in the world!"

Buddy turned to her and smiled. His face, cleaner than she had ever seen it, reflected all the light in the sanctuary. "Me, too," he whispered hoarsely, patting her knee. "I got me a friend, too."

Tears started in her eyes. Suddenly she found herself snuffling. She began to poke into her purse but, before she could find a tissue, Buddy jabbed her arm. He was returning her handkerchief—clean, slightly gray, and very wrinkled, but obviously scrubbed.

She mouthed a thank-you and gently blew her nose. What would James have thought?—Rosamund the star lady, sitting in the second pew with all the poor and needy of the neighborhood, blowing her nose. Or Gail? And the children? She couldn't wait to tell them tomorrow when she saw them.

In the Desert, a Highway

Ko-ko-ko. A pause, then—ko-ko-ko. The knock was no louder than a whisper. Comrade Wong looked at her watch and sighed. Every night at fifteen minutes past twelve, Old Lee tapped his special knock on her dormitory door. And every night when she opened the door, there stood the college night watchman in his faded blue jacket and trousers with a ragged book under his arm, asking her to read to him.

It was dangerous reading the Christian book aloud in the middle of the night. But once last winter, a wind had blown out the flame in her kerosene heater. Old Lee, on his nightly rounds, had smelled the fumes and carried her unconscious body to safety. She had been grateful. She owed him her life, so she had said rashly, "If there is anything I can do for you, comrade . . ."

The next night he had appeared at her door with the book under his arm. "I am a Christian," he had said in his hoarse voice, "but I am an ignorant man and I cannot read the Book.

"Why don't I teach you?" The old man's eyesight was poor and his brain stiff. He could remember a few words, but Chinese characters are intricately made and easily forgotten, even by an agile mind. By summer she gave up all pretense of teaching and simply read to him.

He wanted to begin at the beginning. He marveled over the tales of Genesis. The laws of Exodus and Leviticus had been something of a trial to them both. The rituals of the Hebrews seemed barbaric to Comrade Wong. Once in a while she tried to point out how primitive all these rules were, but Lee simply shook his old head, the gray bristly hair sticking up like dry grass.

"Just read," he said. "Please, sister, just read what it says."

So she'd read on through Numbers and Deuteronomy until she finally got the foolish Israelites out of the wilderness, only in Judges to have them sink into degradation worse than the times before the flood.

"Look at your heroes! They are full of pride and lust and greed," she protested.

He listened gravely as she read of the evil doings of Gideon and Samson and the sons of Samuel, and the mad ravings of Saul the King. When the Book told of David's adultery and murderous act, she thought she saw tears on the old man's face, but he urged her to keep reading.

The best parts were the Psalms. As a teacher of literatures, she liked the poetry, and the old man drank in the words of comfort. They both pretended to ignore the demands of the poets that God slaughter their enemies. It was hard to know exactly who one's enemies were these days. There was great unrest in the city. The two of them did not mention it, but deep inside herself, Comrade Wong was afraid.

By the time the young hoodlums who called themselves Red Guards invaded the campus, Comrade Wong and Old Lee had gotten to Ecclesiastes: "Vanity, vanity, all is vanity . . . " How could all of her ideals be vanity? She had tried with her whole heart to support the revolution. She lived very simply, owning nothing aside from her worn blue garments and a few books, all of which had been approved for their revolutionary thought. She had never married, choosing instead to give her life to teaching the young—to making China a strong and respected nation in the world.

Now these mobs were invading the college grounds, breaking windows, setting fire to library books, until finally some of the students and professors fought back, drove the invaders out, and padlocked the gate against them.

Ko-ko-ko. Silence. *Ko-ko-ko.* Not tonight. Tonight she must decide how to hide her books so they would not be destroyed. She went to the door and cracked it. He stood there but without his book. "I won't keep you long, sister," he said. "But it is getting cold, and I noticed the soles of your shoes are very thin."

"I don't have coupons to buy new shoes," she said. "Times are very hard. We must all bear these minor discomforts for the sake of the revolution."

He nodded. "I made some padded linings for you. If you'll let me borrow your shoes, I'll fit the linings and return your shoes before morning."

"You mustn't bother yourself, comrade. There are others far worse off than I."

"But you have been so kind," he said. "I wanted to make you a small gift"—he gave his sweet, nearly toothless smile—"for Christmas."

She stiffened. The man would get her into trouble yet.

"Would you accept a New Year's gift?" He was like a child, trying so hard to please. How could she offend him?

She handed him her shoes. They were worn straight through as he had observed. "Thank you for your kindness, comrade . . ."

When she opened her door early the next morning, the shoes were there with their new cloth linings and a bright coat of polish. Fortunately they were old and stretched, or the thick new inner soles would have made them too small. They were snug, but the stone floor was no longer so cold beneath her feet.

She crept to the community washroom while it was still dark. She had arisen before dawn because she had to hide her books. When the mob came back, as they surely would, they would finish destroying the library and then ransack the teachers' rooms, destroying whatever threatened them. She had no antiques, no jewelry, not even any banned books. But she did have her literature books. These young zealots were putting out the word that all scholars and students were in fact enemies of the true revolution—that the only book that a true revolutionary needed was the book of Chairman Mao's thoughts. Any other book would lead to false philosophies.

She ripped open her bed quilt and stuffed the small paperback volumes in the middle of the cotton padding. Quickly she sewed the quilt back up. Her fingers were shaking. Although her breath came out in white puffs in the cold room, she perspired as she worked. What about her larger books? Her dictionary? Her anthology of poetry?

Feverishly she gathered them up. They were an awkward, heavy load, but she hurried to the night watchman's door. It was open.

"Sister," he said. "Good morning. Do your new linings fit?"

"They are a great help. Thank you," she said. "May I come in?"

He stepped aside. The room was so tiny that even his meager belongings made it look crowded. "I want to ask you a great favor," she said, looking about for a hiding place.

"Of course, sister." His grin showed his toothless gums.

"Could you—would you hide my books in here? No one would think to look for books in your room."

He grinned even wider than before. "You're right. Everyone knows how ignorant I am." He took the books from her. "Hurry," he said. "The others will be up soon. I'll take care of these for you."

The mob returned about noon. This time there were party officials in the lead and police all around. "We have heard that subversive materials have been harbored here," the local party chairman said.

Faculty and students were herded to the athletic field while the Red Guards went through all the buildings and dormitories. A bonfire was kindled in the midst of the soccer field. Antique furniture, scrolls, and books were brought out and thrown onto the flames. Those in whose rooms the objects were found were separated from the rest of the community. The chairman wrote their names in his notebook.

A great shouting arose. Two of the mob had gone into the night watchman's room, where he pretended to be sleeping. When they tried to drag him out, he clung to the quilts. They were suspicious, and sure enough, the old man was lying on a bed of subversive books. They lifted the books in the air, one by one, before they threw them into the fire.

"See the evil eggs the old one has been trying to hatch!" a young woman screamed.

"The rest of you we only warn," the chairman cried out. "This enemy of the people must be made an example of."

Comrade Wong watched in horror as they stripped off Old Lee's ragged jacket and began to beat him with a thin bamboo stick. She thought a scream would surely escape from her lips each time the stick whacked down on the old man's back. What should she do? Those were her books. He had hidden them for her. Surely he would tell them that.

The college president stepped out from the group and went over to the chairman. "There is some mistake," he said. "Comrade Lee does not know how to read."

A young guard slammed a dunce cap on President Shen's head. He commanded the president to march around the bonfire shouting. "I am a fool! I am a fool!" The mob jeered and screamed with laughter. At last the fire burned out. The teachers and students were dismissed.

The next day Comrade Wong learned that both the president and the night watchman had been taken away. Most of the students packed their bags and went home. "It is nearly the New Year's holiday," they said. The teachers left as well. Comrade Wong had no home to go to—no relative who would take her in.

Night and day she listened for the Red Guards to return. She nursed her fear, because somehow she knew that if she let go of it, even a little, she would be overwhelmed by shame. It was she who had caused the night watchman to be beaten and the president disgraced—both of them to be arrested.

She was almost relieved when the mob came back again, for this time they found the books she had sewn into her quilt and took her away too. She was put in a cattle car with more than thirty other women. Some were prostitutes and thieves, some teachers like herself, others simple women who had no notion what their crime might be.

By the time the doors were flung open again and they were ordered to climb out, the women were filthy and weak to the point of illness. Even the pale winter sun blinded their eyes.

Before them stretched a treeless plain as far as they could see. They must have traveled hundreds of miles into the interior. They stumbled from the train to a line of wooden barracks in the middle of field. There they were at last given water for washing themselves and ordered to come to the dining hall to eat.

"At dawn you will begin work," said a young man, who seemed to be the leader. "We are building a road where no road has ever been built before. To honor the revolution and our beloved chairman, we have the privilege of building a great new highway."

We are too weak to walk, Comrade Wong thought, how can we build a road? But she did as she was told and stumbled to the dining hall. The food was poor, a kind of gruel made of millet, but she ate it. She must regain her strength—if she did not, she would die in this desolate place. She was dimly aware that the hall was crowded. They were not the first workers to be brought here.

She left the table when she finished her gruel, washed her bowl and chopsticks at the common sink, and followed the crowd of women through the darkness to the barracks. She fell asleep at once and dreamed she heard a knocking at the door—*ko-ko-ko* . . . *ko-ko-ko*. She sat bolt upright on the wooden cot and listened, but all she heard was the breathing of the women around her. The next day, as she carried a basket of gravel from the pit to the roadway, she saw him. He was pulling a heavy roller used to smooth the road surface. His face was thinner than she remembered. The night watchman must be at least ten years older than she. Now he looked thirty years older. She went as close to him as she dared.

"I trust that Comrade Lee is in good health," she murmured.

He jerked his head up at her voice and grinned his sweet, toothless smile. "It warms this old heart to see my sister's face once more," he said.

She smiled and nodded her head in a bow. How like him to continue calling her sister—a prerevolutionary greeting. She was absurdly glad to see him. Later that same morning she came upon President Shen as well. He acknowledged her with a stiff nod.

She began looking for them every day. Old Lee would smile across the dining hall at her or nod on the construction site. Despite the poor food and heavy work, she was not unhappy. At the reeducation meeting one night, she confessed to the other women in her little group that she had been a selfish intellectual who had not understood the contribution of the masses to the rebuilding of China. But here, working on the road, she felt she had become a true revolutionary, able at last to understand the teachings of Chairman Mao. She was very grateful.

The group leader was pleased. One day the project head called her to his office—a tiny shack almost filled with an oversized desk. "Comrade Wong," he said, "your confession serves as a fine example to the other women. You are to be congratulated."

"I only spoke what is true," she said. "I am happy to serve the revolution in this place."

She was asked to repeat her confession for several other reeducation groups. At first she was glad to do so, but the night she spoke to the men's group and saw Old Lee and President Shen sitting there, she was embarrassed. They were in this place because of her. Old Lee smiled when she came in, his face so thin that it was like the grin of a skull. The president nodded, but he did not smile. Usually her confession tumbled out like a waterfall, but tonight she stumbled and had to repeat words. She was relieved when it was finally done and she was permitted to leave. She was afraid the project manager would scold her for her poor performance, but instead, as they walked back toward her barracks, he said, "In the group tonight there were two men from your former college, I believe."

"Yes, comrade."

"I hope they will learn from your example."

"They work hard," she said. "I see them on the road. They are good workers, comrade."

"Oh, yes," he said. "They work hard enough. But I see no signs of their renouncing their former counterrevolutionary activity." The leader was fishing for something. "You are aware, I'm sure, that the old one was arrested for hiding right-wing books, and that the younger one was arrested for seeking to defend the wrongdoer."

"I—I heard something of the sort."

"We want you to use your influence with them— persuade them to confess." She was glad it was dark so that he could not see her face. "I don't see how I could be of any help, comrade."

"You are wrong. The old one obviously respects you. I saw his warm greeting. And it is well known that the younger one cares a great deal for the old one. We are going to give you separate housing, comrade," the leader continued. "Then your former colleagues can visit you. You can talk to them, show them the virtue of confessing their past errors and embracing with a full heart the teachings of our chairman."

So Comrade Wong was given a little shack of her own and a new, bright red copy of the teachings of Chairman Mao. No longer did she have to carry baskets of gravel. She was a supervisor on the road. But not even she knew where the road was going. It began abruptly in the middle of nowhere, and they were building it inch by inch toward the setting sun.

Old Lee continued to pull a roller. It was work for an ox or a mule, but they had neither. The president was one of the men who raked the gravel in an even layer after it was dumped on the roadway by the women. Sometimes, if he finished raking before a new load arrived, he would run to where Old Lee was straining at the roller's ropes and help the old man pull. Perhaps, as supervisor, Comrade Wong should have reprimanded him for leaving his own post, but she did not.

One evening after supper the two of them appeared at her door. As always, Old Lee smiled broadly at the sight of her. The president's face was stern. It was he who spoke.

"The project leader said you wished to see us."

So, the time had come. She stepped aside to let them enter her room. There was only one chair. She motioned for the president to sit on it, but he nodded for Old Lee to take the chair and he himself sat down on the floor. Old Lee grinned, shook his head, and sat down on the floor as well. Comrade Wong perched on the edge of her cot and stared at the empty chair. She did not know how to begin.

"This brings back happy times," the old man said. "Miss Wong tried to teach me to read, you know."

"No," said the president. "I did not know." He looked a bit less stern.

Now he will tell, thought Comrade Wong, wondering who might be listening outside the door, but the old man said nothing more.

She stared at the beaten earth floor of her little shack. How could she persuade them to confess when it was her wrongdoing for which they had been brought to this place of exile?

At last the president said, "Comrade Wong, I think it is your duty to speak to us about reeducation. Comrade Lee and I are suspected of harboring right-wing religious beliefs."

She looked up in surprise.

"After he was taken to the police station and stripped, they found pages of the Christian Bible sewn up in his padded jacket," he said. "Of course, he would never have been taken to the station if"—his voice dropped to a whisper—"if it were not for the books found in his room."

Her face was hot. "If you would only say in your reeducation group that your past thinking was mistaken and that you are eager to be reeducated . . ." She heard the pleading tone in her voice and felt shame.

"How can an old fool like me be reeducated, sister? I was never educated to begin with."

"Perhaps," said the president, "he could tell how he came to have right-wing books in his room."

"Yes," Comrade Wong said weakly, "he could do that."

"I can't confess to having right-wing books in my room. How can I know if a book is right wing, left wing, or tail wing? I can't read a character. You know that as well as anyone, sister."

"*Comrade*," she said.

"Oh, yes. *Comrade.*"

"You see, Comrade Wong. Your cause is hopeless. Tell the project leader you tried, but it is hopeless," said the president.

"But what about you, Comrade Shen? Surely you are not hopeless."

"I was detained and sent here for reeducation because I made an inflammatory public statement: 'Comrade Lee does not know how to read.' How can I repent for saying publicly what is absolutely true?"

"Perhaps there is something in your past life, unrelated to Comrade Lee . . ." She did not ask him if he had ever been a Christian. She did not ask them anything for fear they would think her an informer.

"Good night, comrade," the president was saying. "I am sorry we have been such trouble to you." She could tell by his eyes that he already considered her an informer.

"It will take time," she told the project leader. "The old one is a hard-headed peasant and the younger one feels a certain loyalty to him."

Comrade Wong suggested a human chain for passing baskets of gravel from the pit to the roadway, which made the procedure more efficient. She was declared "People's Hero" for the month of August. Otherwise, August was a terrible month. The heat burned the crops in the fields and there was no rain.

She saw Old Lee fall down. She was sure it was heatstroke and told President Shen and another worker to carry him to the barracks and take care of him. When he came back to work the next morning, he was so weak that, pull and tug as he did, the roller would not move.

Shen came up to her. "With Comrade Wong's permission, I will help Comrade Lee pull the roller."

"You cannot do both your work and his."

"Let me try."

"No," she said. "I will rake today."

At last, with September, the rain came. She heard it *tung tung* on the tin roof and then thunder down like horses on a gallop. It continued through the next day. They tried to work on the road but sank to their ankles in mud. Even the project leader saw it was useless and ordered them back to the barracks.

She was cleaning the mud off her shoes when she realized that the cloth covering the lining that Old Lee had made for her last winter was worn through to the paper core. She held the lining up to her small kerosene lamp. A single word of two characters showed through the hole— *gung luh*—highway. She smiled. Curious to know what the article, probably from an old newspaper, was saying about a highway and, hungry for something to read, anything, she stuck her index finger into the hole and pushed the cloth up a bit. "Make straight in the desert" . . . she pulled the cloth down . . . "a highway for our God."

Her heart froze. She took the tiny pair of scissors from the sewing kit she had been issued as a supervisor and clipped the stitches that bound the lining. Her hand was shaking so much that the task took twice as long as it should have. The cloth and paper were wet. She had to be very careful. But at last she could read the top layer of printing. "Comfort, comfort my people, says your God. Speak comfortably to Jerusalem, and cry unto her that her warfare is accomplished, that her iniquity is pardoned, for she has received of the Lord's hand double for all her sins. The voice of him that cries in the wilderness, Prepare the way of the Lord, make straight in the desert a highway for our God . . ."

She didn't know whether to laugh or be angry. All these months she had thought he was suffering for her, while all the time she had been unwittingly hiding pages from his Book, walking on them every day. Suppose she had been caught? His punishment would be nothing compared to what she might receive. That pose of being an old fool, when all the time . . . Quickly she cut a patch from the seam of her jacket and mended the hold in the lining. No one must ever know.

When the sun came out at last, it was on a scene of devastation. The stretch of highway they had built so painstakingly over the last nine months had washed away. Most of the gravel had been swallowed up by a sea of mud. They must begin all over again.

Between the prolonged drought and the flood, the local crops were ruined. There was no harvest, and as the days grew colder, the weaker ones among them began to fall ill. Comrade Wong spent her days supervising a dwindling crew and her nights nursing the sick in the women's barracks.

One morning Old Lee did not appear. President Shen was pulling the roller and then going behind it to rake. She took the rake from his hands. He did not thank her but he did not object.

After a supper of thin gruel, she checked on the women who were sick. The flimsy barracks were as cold as the outdoors. She cautioned the women to sleep in all the clothes they owned and then went to her own shack to fall into exhausted sleep. *Ko-ko-ko . . . ko-ko-ko.* Was it a dream? She jumped up and opened the door. There stood the form of Old Lee, thin as a wraith, swaying in the doorway. He began to cough. She pulled him in and shut the door. There was no kerosene for the lamp, so she lit her one candle. He bent over in a fit of coughing, beads of sweat gleaming on his forehead in the pale light. She grabbed the quilt off the cot, wrapped it around him, and eased him into the chair. "You shouldn't be walking about," she scolded. "You'll catch pneumonia."

He smiled through his coughing. "You are always so kind to me, sister."

She shook her head impatiently. "What are you doing out here in the middle of the night, comrade?"

"It is nearly Christmas," he said. "I wanted to give you a present."

"You gave me one last year," she said. "The linings for my shoes, remember?"

"But I never had a chance to tell you," he said. "The real present was not the linings, it was inside the linings."

"I—I found it," she said. Her face grew hot in the darkness. "I thought you might be using my shoes as your hiding place."

"No," he said. "I swear. It was for you. I can't read. I wanted you to have it in case we could not read together anymore. But there were too many pages. I could only put a little bit in for you."

"Forgive me," she said. She could not bear to look at his

sweating face, so thin and earnest. "You have been kinder to me than I have to you."

"Oh, sister, you are always kind to me."

"My books." She choked out the words. "You are suffering because of me. It is not right. Tomorrow, I will explain—"

"No!" He dropped his voice. "You must never say a word. These hard times will pass, and then China will need you to teach again. I am only a night watchman." He reached out his hand. "Promise me this one thing before I die."

"You must not die. Not for me."

"We must all die, sister. I am well content. I go to be with Jesus. Just give me this one gift. Promise me you will not speak of this."

She could feel her heart swelling and aching inside her chest.

"Promise me?" he asked again. He wiped the sweat from his forehead with the back of his hand.

"Yes, yes, comrade. Now you must go. It isn't safe for you to be out in this cold."

The next day the whole project was ordered to remain in the dining hall after breakfast. Last night, the project leader informed them, Comrade Lee had been caught near the road. It was obvious that he meant to run away. "For his own good and the good of the group he must be punished."

Two of the supervisors stripped off the old man's jacket and began to beat him. Comrade Wong closed her eyes and put the back of her hand against her mouth to keep from screaming. She had promised him, she kept saying to herself. She had promised.

"Stop!" a voice cried. Comrade Wong opened her eyes. President Shen had covered Old Lee's back with his own body. "He was delirious last night. Can't you see? He's burning up with fever. Leave him alone!" But they pulled the president away and finished the beating.

She tried to speak to Shen later in the day, but each time he just looked at her tight-lipped, turned his back, and walked away. Finally she grabbed his arm. "You must tell me how he is!"

The president's eyes flashed. "He is dying. What did you expect?"

"Please. I beg you, bring him to my room tonight. I want to nurse him."

"You?"

"Please. I must do something."

"Aren't you afraid?" The tone was bitter.

"Yes," she said. "Of course I'm afraid. But it doesn't matter. Please bring him."

Late that night the two of them, Comrade Wong and the president, put Old Lee on her cot and covered him with all three of their quilts.

Even in his fever, he was smiling widely. "What friends God gives me," he said. "What friends."

"I have a present for you," she said. "I've taken the linings apart so I can read to you."

She brought her chair close to the cot.

"This is wonderful," the old man said. "I couldn't have dreamed of such a present." He motioned weakly for the president to sit down on the edge of the cot.

She began to read. "'Comfort, comfort my people, says your God. Speak comfortably to Jerusalem . . .'"

"Ahh," the old man sighed. "I have never heard this part before."

"'The voice of him that cries in the wilderness. Prepare

the way of the Lord, make straight in the desert a highway for our God.'"

Old Lee struggled to sit up. "Do you hear? It is a word for us, here in this place. We are road builders."

"Oh, my elder brother, don't you see? It is you who have built the highway." She eased him down and covered him again. "Now, truly, you must rest."

"After I die I can rest," he said. "Please keep reading, sister."

But she was afraid that if she opened her mouth she would weep, so she handed the shoe-shaped page to the president and he leaned toward the flickering candle and continued:

"'Every valley shall be exalted, and every mountain and hill shall be made low and the crooked shall be made straight, and the rough places plain;

"And the glory of the Lord shall be revealed, and all flesh shall see it together: for the mouth of the Lord has spoken it . . .'"

On the Night of His Birth: Mary's Story

Sing out, my soul, the wonder . . .

They are gone now, those shepherds, smelling of their sheep and rubbing their broad, country faces with chapped and grimy hands, their eyes still dazed with angel light.

"Please, can we touch him?"

How could I say no? God is the host of this strange celebration at which I, too, am guest.

"Hail, most favored one!" He spoke to me. God summoned me, as though to play a divine joke on a prideful world. Pity Isaiah. When that noble prophet sang of David's line, could he have dreamed of me?

Not even my mother could do that. When I returned so full of joy from Elizabeth's house, she met me with angry tears. "Was it a soldier on the road?" she asked. My own mother—who once held me, just as I hold this child of mine.

My father did not speak, but I could see the questions in his eyes. Does she lie? Has she gone mad? And which is better, there being no comfort in either answer? They are sick with shame, for they are simple, pious people who care what the neighbors say.

Even Joseph—but how could I blame him? An angel come to Nazareth? God's Holy Spirit come to me, a nothing child, a poor man's girl? King David's mighty shout shrunk to a whisper in our peasant blood?

But God is good. Joseph had his own stern visitant. And though my man sang no magnificat, he did obey. God give him joy for that. And there he sits, meaning to keep watch, his head a stone upon his chest. Not knowing—he trusts. My heart swelled to feel his pain, his puzzlement, and then, tonight, to see the gentle way he washed the son who was not his.

The boy stirs in his sleep. I have fed him and he is satisfied. Can you believe it? God's anointed one upon my breast, with milk, just there, at the corner of his tiny mouth.

His hair is black and thick and stands up like shocks of weed upon his head. I try to smooth it with my lips, but it springs back, refusing my correction. I laugh aloud.

My Joseph moans. I have disturbed his rest, but how can I be silent? Every part of me shouts and sings. I have brought a child into the world. From my own flesh has come this perfect thing.

A little hand pokes through the bands. Unpracticed as I am, I have not wrapped him well; he moves within the clothes to nestle into the curve of my body. We are almost one again. But now I can see him. I can touch him. I can nurse him and care for him.

He is God's. I know that. The word of angels earthed in my cousin's cry of praise; and the rough fingers of the herdsmen smoothing this down cheek in wordless worship.

He is God's, and God's ways are past all my understanding. I cannot see the man he will become, or even the ruddy-faced boy. I do not know what God will ask of him— or me. I am the handmaid of the Lord; my son, his servant. Dare I say? My son, his son.

But now, this morning, the light breaks. The world wakes to a day that has never been, and I hold my baby in my arms, and that alone is miracle beyond belief. Sing out, my soul, the wonder . . .

 # Angels and Other Strangers

M inutes after the letter came from Arlene, Jacob set out walking for Washington. He wondered how long it would take him to get there. Before the truck died, he could make it in an hour, but he'd never tried to walk it. At sixty he knew that he didn't have the endurance that he had once had, but he was still a strong man. Perhaps he could get there by morning if he kept a steady pace. Or if he could at least reach a place where there was a bus, he could ride as far as the few bills in his pocket could take him.

Arlene needed him, so he would go to her if he had to walk every step of the way. Arlene, his baby granddaughter— it seemed as if he had only just stopped bouncing her on his knee—was going to have a baby herself. She was alone and scared in the city and wanted her granddaddy, so he put on his dead wife's overcoat and then his own and started out. The two coats protected him from the wet snow, but his wife's was too small and cut under his arms. "I'm coming, Arlene baby," he said to the country road. "I'm going to be with you for Christmas."

How wonderful it would be, thought Jacob, if someone stopped and offered him a ride. Occasionally a car would pass, even on this almost deserted stretch. Once he almost raised his arm to try to wave one down, but thought better of it. Who would give a ride to a black man on a lonely road? He could hope in the Lord, but he'd better rely on his own two feet. No rest, as the Good Book said, for the weary.

In Washington, Julia Thompson was humming as she worked. Why was she so happy? Because she had two beautiful children and a loving husband. Because Walter, her husband, would be singing at the Christmas Eve service, and she always felt so proud and was thrilled by his voice. Because it was nearly Christmas. Yes, of course, all those things, but, hallelujah, it was the first Christmas since she'd known Walter that she hadn't had to deal with his Aunt Patty.

Aunt Patty was Walter's only living relative. Some respect was due her for his sake, but nothing ever went quite right with Aunt Patty. The best years were the ones when she had simply grumbled her way through the celebration, taking the edge off everyone else's enjoyment. But the last three years, she'd managed to orchestrate a series of disasters, though how could you blame an old lady for falling down on the church walk just before the Christmas Eve service and having to be rushed to the hospital with a broken hip? Perhaps Aunt Patty should have known enough not to give a two-year-old a teddy bear with button eyes which he could and would immediately pull out and swallow, but she had not known, and it had meant that they had spent Christmas Day with Kevin in the emergency room. Last year, despite Julia's apprehension, everything had gone well, until they, with great excitement, told her the news that they were expecting another child. Aunt Patty, who had never before revealed a social conscience, suddenly burst into a lament for all the starving people in the world. Here they were, gorging themselves and daring to be happy, while at the same time producing still another baby to crowd out the hungry millions.

But this year, despite Walter's urgings, Aunt Patty had decided not to make the thirty-mile trip into the city. The weather was uncertain, and her bursitis had been acting up. Julia cleaned the house and shopped and baked with an energy she hadn't possessed since before Jenny was born. She even had strength left over to take the children on long walks and read aloud to Kevin. It was going to be a wonderful Christmas.

Julia put the baby down for a nap and then took Kevin up on her own bed and began reading to him. Ordinarily, Kevin loved being read to, but today he squirmed and wriggled straight through "The Night Before Christmas." "My, you're fidgety," she said.

"Little boys are supposed to be fidgety," he said with dignity.

She hugged him close. "Now this is the story from the Bible about when Jesus was born. Try to listen, all right?"

"All right."

She read him the story of Mary and Joseph coming down from Nazareth to Bethlehem, stopping to explain about the taxes, the crowded inn, and the manger, going on to the shepherds in the field.

"'And, lo, the angel of the Lord came upon them, and the glory of the Lord'—well, it's like a great light, Kevin— 'shone round about them: and they were sore afraid. And the angel said unto them, Fear not . . .'"

"Why were they afraid, Mommy?"

"I don't know—I guess the light and the strangeness. They'd never seen a real angel before."

He seemed satisfied. She read on, and since he was beginning to nod, she finished the whole chapter in a quiet voice until he was sound asleep. Julia propped pillows around him and went into the kitchen to clean up the lunch things and get ready for the evening. It was then that she discovered that they had no tangerines. Perhaps she was being silly, Kevin was only four and Jenny scarcely five months, but a Christmas stocking without a tangerine in the toe seemed somehow incomplete, and Julia was determined that this be a perfect Christmas. She got Becky, the teenager from next door, to baby-sit long enough to let her drive to the grocery store to pick up a few. She was home within twenty minutes.

"Everything quiet?" she asked the sitter. "Sure. Fine. Your aunt called."

Julia's heart sank. "She said to tell you she'd changed her mind and would Mr. Thompson please come pick her up."

Julia should have asked Becky to stay with the children and gone then and there to get Aunt Patty, but she didn't. She paid Becky a dollar and sent her home before she tried to figure out what to do. Could she pretend she never got the message? No. She dialed Walter's office, looking at her watch as she did so. It was now three thirty. If he could leave Washington right away, he could drive the thirty-odd miles to Bethel, pick up Aunty Patty, and get back in time for his rehearsal. But when his secretary finally answered, it was to say that there had been an accident in the plant in Virginia, and that Walter had gone out to see about it. If he called in, she would have him call home.

There was no way Walter could get Aunt Patty. Even if she could reach him on his cell phone, he was too far away to make the trip to pick us his aunt and get back in time for his choir rehearsal. There was no way to get Aunt Patty today, unless—Reluctantly she dialed the neighbors. No, Becky had already gone out with friends. She'd tried, Julia told herself. She really had. No one would expect her to put two sleeping children in the car and drive halfway across Maryland in bad weather.

The phone rang. "Julia?" It was, of course, Aunty Patty. "I want you just to forget my message. You mustn't bother Walter about me at such a busy time. It looks like snow anyhow. It would be ridiculous to come all the way out here."

Kevin came padding down the hall in his sock feet. "Who's that, Mommy?" he asked, still half asleep.

"Aunt Patty," Julia said.

"Aunt Patty!" His face lit up. "She's coming for Christmas!"

"Now I don't want you to feel bad," Aunt Patty was saying. Just forget all about me and have a wonderful—"

"Aunt Patty," Julia broke in wearily, "we'll be there to get you as soon as we can."

There was a silence at the other end of the line. "Well, I think it's ridiculous to try to make it out here in this weather, but . . . Well, all right. Since you insist."

Julia woke the baby and bundled both children into the car. It was already getting dark and snowing lightly, but she couldn't honestly say that the roads were dangerous. Even driving slowly, she could have plenty of time to get out to Aunt Patty's house in the country and back in time for the service. Of course she hadn't counted on the crowded interstate on Christmas Eve afternoon. They alternately crawled and sat, motors idling, horns honking about them.

On the back seat Jenny slept while Kevin chattered away. He was so excited about getting his Aunt Patty that he sang songs about it, substituting Aunt Patty for Santa Claus. I ought to deserve some credit, Julia thought, that despite everything, I've never turned Kevin against her.

It was nearly five before they were off the main highway and moving at a decent rate of speed. If the visibility had been really poor or the road icy, Julia would have turned around for home even then. But there was no way she could escape this journey now without disappointing her little boy and making herself feel like Scrooge incarnate.

They were dangerously low on gas, but there was a station just this side of Aunt Patty's place where she could fill up, so she pushed on. When they got there, though, the station was closed for the holiday, so she drove on to Aunt Patty's house.

"Just wait with Jenny, Kevin. I'll run in and get Aunt Patty, and we'll be right back." She dashed from the driveway to the back door and banged. It was bitter cold, though the snow was slackening. She tried the door. It fell open. "Aunt Patty?" she called in the hallway. One of Aunt Patty's cats came bouncing down the steps, meowing menacingly. "Aunt Patty?" She was seized with a sudden panic that the old woman might be lying somewhere in the house, ill or worse. Then her eye fell on the note on the kitchen table.

"Walter," it said. "I've just run up to Gertrude's for a minute. You can pick me up there or wait here for me. I won't be long. Love." Walter, were he here, might know who

Gertrude was, but Julia had no notion. She wouldn't even know how to look her up in the phone book.

She went back to the car.

"Where's Aunt Patty?" asked Kevin. Where indeed was Aunt Patty?

"She went to see a friend and is coming back soon. We'll go put some gas in the car. By the time we get back, she'll probably be here."

"Why'd she go away? Didn't she know we were coming?"

Julia started the engine and began backing down the drive. She was not going to ruin Christmas by losing her temper.

"Why, Mommy?"

"I don't know, Kevin. She didn't tell me."

"Did you see her?"

"No. She left a note." Addressed to Walter, naturally.

"What did the note say?"

"She just said she was going out for a few minutes and would be right back."

"Why?"

"Kevin!"

"Why'd you yell at me, Mommy?"

"Please, Kevin. I've got to watch the road." Where in the world was the nearest gas station? One that would still be open at five thirty on Christmas Eve? There was a housing development with a shopping center somewhere about—she had driven there once with Walter—if she could remember the road to take to cut over to it. Aunt Patty's road was a narrow two-lane country road with very few houses. The windshield wipers pushed the snow aside, and she sat hunched forward, peering out into the path of the headlights, not daring to glance at the gas gauge.

In the darkness, nothing looked familiar. She rarely came

out here, and when she did, Walter always drove. She should have stayed and waited for Aunt Patty, but it was too late now to try to turn around and get back.

"Why are you stopping the car, Mommy?"

Julia got her purse off the passenger seat to fish out her phone when she remembered. The battery had been low. She'd left the phone in the kitchen charger. Julia put her head down on the wheel. She was not going to panic. She had two children to look after. She had to think clearly.

The baby woke up and began to scream.

"The baby woke up, Mommy."

"I know, sweetheart."

"Why'd you stop the car?"

"Don't get upset, Kevin. We've just run out of gas. Everything will be all right. Just don't get upset."

"I'm not upset. The baby's upset. I'm fidgety."

"Well, you can get out of your seat for a while." She reached back and undid his seat belt. He clambered happily into the front seat.

"Oh, tuna fish," he cursed, four-year-old style. "It's stopped snowing."

Julia took Jenny out of the car bed. One thing at a time. First, the baby must be fed. As she nursed the baby, she began to sing to entertain Kevin, who was jealous that his sister could have her supper while he could not.

They were singing about glories streaming from heaven afar when Kevin spotted the light ahead. "Look, Mommy!"

Jacob had first seen the headlights come quickly over a rise far down the road and then as quickly disappear. He kept walking, swinging his huge flashlight as he went, expecting them to reappear at any moment. Not that it mattered. The car was heading the wrong way for him anyhow, even if by some miracle it was someone who would consider giving him a ride. At least it had stopped snowing. Just then the beam of his flashlight caught a car sitting in the darkness. There were people inside. He hesitated a moment. What if it were a trick? For himself he didn't mind dying. Lord knew he was ready to go, but Arlene needed him now. He had to get to Washington. Yet here, perhaps, was somebody else in need. He started across the road, heading for the driver's side of the car.

"Look, Mommy!" Kevin said again. "Glory streams from heaven afar." A strong bright light moved over the rise and down the hill toward them. Julia stopped singing and watched it come. Finally, behind the light, she could make out the tall bulging shadow of a man. She checked quickly to make sure all the doors were locked, took the baby off her breast, and straightened her clothes with a shaking hand. The light was coming straight for her window. Her eyes blinked to shut out the brightness, and when she opened them, a huge black face, which seemed to fill the side window of the small car, was there within inches of her cheek. She pulled back. The man tapped on the window with a worn brown glove that showed the tips of his fingers, and said something through the glass. Julia squeezed the baby tighter and stared straight ahead.

Kevin leaned across her and banged the glass. "Hi!" he said.

"Hi yourself."

Out of the corner of her eye Julia could see the black face smiling broadly. The chin was covered with silver bristles and several teeth were missing. She tried to grab at Kevin to shush him.

"Need some help?" This time the man was shouting as though to make sure she could hear him plainly through the window, but she refused to turn her head.

"Mommy, why don't you answer the nice man?"

"Shh, Kevin. We don't know what he wants."

"He wants to know if we need some help."

The man leaned close to the glass and shouted again. "Don't be afraid, little lady."

"You hear that, Mommy?"

"Kevin, please."

"But, Mommy, he said, 'Don't be afraid!' That's what *angels* say."

"Kevin, no!"

But before she could catch him, Kevin had slid across the seat, pulled up the button, opened the door, and jumped out of the car. The man immediately started around to meet him.

"Don't you touch my child!" Julia screamed, twisting awkwardly from under the wheel, still clutching the baby.

"You don't want him running out into the road, do you, lady?"

"No. No. Thank you." She took Kevin's hand.

"I saw your car and figured you was in trouble."

There was no way to ignore him now. But she had to be careful. He was over six feet tall and obviously strong. The police-pamphlet directions flashed across her brain: *Be sure to look carefully at your assailant so you can give an accurate description to the police later.* If there was a later. Oh, God, don't let him hurt me. Don't let him hurt the children.

"We ran out of gas," said Kevin.

Why was she so afraid of him? He, Jacob, who had never

willfully hurt the least one of God's creatures—couldn't she tell by looking at him that he only wanted to help? Even the child could see that. He stretched out his hand to put it on the boy's head, but seeing the look in the woman's eyes, he brought it back.

"Your old car's got a empty belly, huh?"

The boy giggled. "Me, too," he said. "I haven't even had my supper."

"Well, we gotta do something about that. I passed a gas station a while back," Jacob said to the woman. "You don't have a can, do you?"

She shook her head. She seemed to be shivering.

"You better get back in the car and try to stay warm." He turned and started back up the hill, sighing as he retraced the descent of a few minutes before. It seemed to have grown steeper. But, at least, praise the Lord, the snow had stopped and the sky was clearing.

"Wait," she called after him. "You'll need some money."

"I got some," Jacob said. He didn't want to waste time and energy going back down the hill.

Suppose he never came back? Would they grow cold and sleepy and freeze out here in the middle of nowhere on Christmas Eve? Well, Aunt Patty, you will have certainly beaten your own record this year—even Christmas morning in the emergency room will pale in comparison. And then suppose he did come back?

What did he want? He could have just taken her purse and run, if money was what he wanted. But of course it was the car he was after, so he could get away faster—but she tried not to think of that.

"I think we should sing some more songs," Kevin said. "I might forget about my tummy."

Julia was glad for the diversion. They sang through every carol she knew, even la-la-ing through unfamiliar verses. Then they sang all the songs on Kevin's favorite records, then another round of Christmas carols. Until at long last they saw the light coming over the hill.

"Here comes the glory light," said Kevin.

This time when the man came to her window, she rolled it down. "Would you hold the flashlight for me while I pour the gas in?" he asked.

Trembling, she laid Jenny down in the car bed and went around to the tank.

He handed her his big torch, which she tried to hold steady as he poured.

"Well, thank you," Julia said when he had finished, keeping her voice cool. "Let me pay you something for all your trouble."

Jacob looked at her. She was going to give him some money and drive off. He had given her nearly an hour of his time and far more of his energy than he could spare. There was no way she could pay him for that. But she had already gone to the front seat and gotten her purse, the little boy scampering around her at every step.

"That's all right," he said. "Forget it."

She stuck a few bills out at him. "But I owe you for the gas."

"I—uh—do need to return the can. If you could give me a ride down the road and back. . . ."

She nodded.

He could tell by her eyes that she didn't want him in her car, but, Lord, she owed him that much. He decided to ignore her eyes.

"Well, old man," he said to the child, "let's see if we can

get this old buggy going." He took the boy around and put him in his seat, letting the child tell him how to buckle the belt, and then climbed into the front seat.

The woman put her purse down between them and buckled herself in. Jacob looked down at the purse and then realized she had caught him looking. He quickly shifted his gaze. "Just down the road a couple miles or so," he said.

Within ten minutes they were at the lighted station. She gave the can back to the attendant and asked him to fill the tank. She saw his eyes question the presence of the man on the seat beside her. Should she try to signal for help? It seemed too foolish. The man had done nothing except try to help her—so far. She at least owed him a ride home on this freezing night.

"We come to get my Aunt Patty to take her home for Christmas." Oh, Kevin.

"Is that a fact? Where's your home, old man?"

Don't answer him, Kevin. But of course Kevin, who had memorized his full address at nursery school, recited it in a proud singsong: "Thirteen-oh-six Essex Street Northwest, Washington, D. C. Two-oh-oh-one-six."

"My, you're one smart boy."

"I know," said Kevin.

I could get a ride all the way to Washington tonight, Jacob said to himself. All I have to do is ask. But he couldn't make himself say the words. If the woman had seemed in the least bit friendly, the least bit trusting, he would have asked her. But how could he ask a favor of a person who thought he was going to grab her purse or hurt her kids?

She had started the car and was pulling out of the station. "Where shall I let you off?" she asked.

It was his chance to tell her. She owed him something,

didn't she? And Arlene was waiting, not even knowing if he had gotten her letter.

"Just down the road," he mumbled. "Just anywhere."

They drove past the place where they had met, but he gave no sign of wanting to be let out, so Julia drove on. She couldn't just stop in the middle of nowhere and order him out. What should she do? They went on until she could see Aunt Patty's house ablaze with light. Aunt Patty was home. Thank God for small blessings.

"Here's where my Aunt Patty lives," Kevin told the stranger.

"Is that a fact?"

The problem of how to get Aunt Patty without leaving the children alone in the car with the man solved itself. Aunt Patty came rushing out of the house, coat and suitcase flying. She had obviously been watching for the car. When she saw Julia at the wheel, she was furious. "Where have you been?" she demanded. "You're going to make me miss the music."

Julia opened her mouth to defend herself, but at the same moment her passenger got out of the car. He stood there tall and straight against the starry winter sky.

"Mercy!" Aunt Patty screamed. "What in the world?"

"He's our angel, Aunt Patty. Our Christmas angel."

"Don't be ridiculous, Kevin."

Ridiculous indeed! All Julia's fears evaporated in a puff of anger. How dare Aunt Patty call it ridiculous? The man had been an angel. She leaned across the seat and called out, "Would you mind squeezing in back with the children?"

Even in the darkness she thought she could see him smile.

"Get in, Aunt Patty," she commanded, "or you'll make us miss the music."

A little farther down the road she turned to him. "How far can I take you?"

"I need to go all the way to Washington," he said.

"Oh, goody!" cried Kevin. "Then you can go to church with us! We never had a real angel in our church before."

He patted the boy's knee. "Can't make it this time, old man," he said. "I got to see this lonesome little girl. Cheer her up for Christmas."

"Angels are really busy, aren't they?"

Jacob laughed, a great rich sound which filled the car. "Yeah," he said. "We keep busy, but it's mighty pleasant work."

Aunt Patty may have said something like "ridiculous," but Julia chose joyfully to ignore it. This was going to be a perfect Christmas.

Merit Badges

S couts," Mrs. Bushey was saying, "we are entirely too involved in ourselves." It was all I could do to keep from snickering out loud. I didn't dare look at Amy. We'd both collapse. Mrs. Bushey always said "scouts" not "girls" or "kids" like a normal grown-up, or "students" like a teacher.

How did the woman ever get to be a scout leader, anyhow? I wondered. Well, of course, Judy quit to have a baby. That's how. They were desperate for somebody—anybody—to take over. But where would you dig up someone like Bushey? All of us called her Bushey behind her back. It absolutely fit. She had a bad home permanent that frizzed all over her strange little round head and she never shaved her legs. She was a sight.

"What?" I hadn't been paying attention. Apparently,

Bushey had been plowing ahead with some harebrained scheme (no pun intended).

"Are we agreed then, Scout Hensen?"

"Sure, okay." What in the world had I agreed to do? I'd have to ask Amy later.

"Then here are the names of the residents and a little bit about each. We won't be able to make special friends with every one. We just wouldn't have the time, what with our busy school and activity schedules, would we?" Why did Bushey always say "we?" Didn't the woman know any other pronouns" *Residents?* I suddenly heard the word. What was Bushey talking about? What residents?

"There," said Bushey happily, "we have made a start in caring. We scouts must endeavor to be caring persons, mustn't we?"

The ten of us somehow got through Bushey's closing ceremony of the scout pledge and a song about friendship that must have been written about the time of the *Mayflower.*

We stumbled out of the dark church basement into the late afternoon sunshine, but not before every other member of the troop was looking at me, their smirks exploding into shrieks. "Ah-ha, Kate, Bushwhacked, Bushwhacked." Amy had made up that term for anyone in the troop who let Bushey sucker her into something. "What do you mean? I didn't get Bushwhacked. I wanted to." "You're lying." Amy stared at me.

Now I was caught. I couldn't admit that I had no idea what I'd promised to do. "Kate! You know perfectly well what happened when Judy took us there last Christmas."

"Christmas?" Here was a clue.

"The caroling. The 'disaster of the decade!'" That's what Judy had called our attempt to cheer up the residents at Logan Manor. My skin began to creep. Had I promised to do something at the manor?

"That was just one crazy old woman," I said nervously.

"Sto------op!" Amy yelled. "Stop the noise!" imitating the old woman who had raced out of her room while we were singing "Silent Night." We'd been scared silly at the time, but now it was one of our group jokes. Whenever we wanted to make each other giggle, somebody would begin imitating the old lady who had driven us out of the nursing home where we had gone to carol last Christmas.

All the others joined in. "Sto------op! Stop the noise!"

"So?" I pretended not to care. "She's not the only person there. I don't have to try to cheer her up. I can choose someone else."

"Aren't we a *good* scout?" Laura pinched her mouth in a perfect imitation of Bushey.

"Shut up, Laura," I muttered. I could just see Bushey's frizzed head coming up the steps out of the basement.

It was bedtime before I looked at the list Bushey had given me. It was typed, but obviously by someone who hadn't mastered the delete button. There were twenty-six names on the list. All women. All old. There were stars beside about ten of the names. At the bottom it said: "*These residents have no one who comes to visit on a regular basis." There were four names that had double stars. "**These residents have no visitors."

Suddenly I felt freezing cold. I put on my bathrobe and went downstairs. My mother was still in the kitchen packing lunches for the next day. "Mom?"

"Katie. I thought you were already in bed."

"I'm just going."

She looked at me for a minute. "Is something the matter?"

"No." I felt silly and about four years old. "I guess—I guess I just wanted to come down and make sure you were here," I said.

She smiled. "Where else would I be, Pumpkin?" It was a baby name she hardly ever used anymore.

I kissed her cheek. "I love you, Mom."

"I love you, too. Now off to bed with you."

It was a couple of days before I looked at the list again. By this time I'd decided several things. One, I would not choose anyone who *never* had visitors. That was likely to get me the stop-the-noise crazy one in that bunch. If I was going to do this—and none of my friends believed for a minute that I had the nerve—I would have to choose someone who wouldn't run me off or scare me to death.

On the other hand, it didn't seem quite fair to choose someone who already had regular visitors. That left the ten one-starred residents. The ones on this list with scary descriptions like "probably Alzheimer's" or "unable to speak" or "deaf" I crossed off. We were a scout, not a doctor or a psychologist, right? We were not going to bite off more than we could chew and give our friends the satisfaction of seeing us fail.

This got the list down to three residents. I chose Mildred Hull (husband deceased, no children, likes to play cards) because if you couldn't think of anything to say, you could always play cards. And besides, if the woman could play cards, she couldn't be totally off her rocker.

Monday afternoon was scout meeting. I was determined to make my first visit before then, but Sunday came and I still hadn't gone. I was tempted to ask Mom to go with me. But she and Dad had promised to do something at church. I dragged out my scout uniform, which had been in the closet since the "disaster of the decade." The sleeves cut me under the arms, and I looked really doofy. But I told myself it was like wearing a costume for Halloween. You could be someone else dressed up. I guess I needed the protection.

At the desk near the front door was a very skinny woman with an enormous head of hair that made her look lopsided. I bit the inside of my cheek to keep from giggling.

"Yes, honey?" the woman said. She didn't look like the kind of woman that would call you honey, but never mind. I cleared my throat. "I'm here to see Mrs. Hull," I said.

"Who?"

"Mrs. Mildred Hull." From barely a croak I went to a boom and the woman ducked her head as if to say, "They're deaf, not me."

But all she said was: "Is Mildred expecting you?"

"Oh." I should have called. It was a little late to think of that now. "I don't think so. I'm Kathryn Hensen—I'm—from the Girl Scouts."

"Where is your leader?" That's what the aliens always want to know. I shrugged. Let her think my leader forgot or something.

She considered me. "Well," she said finally, "why don't you wait here while I go and see what Mildred's up to. A lot of our little people take a nap in the afternoon." Her voice dropped to a whisper as though she was letting me in on a big secret.

There was nothing to do but stand there by the desk while old women shuffled past, staring me up and down as if I was an endangered species in the zoo. The label of my uniform scratched the back of my neck, and I could feel the seams cutting the flesh under my arms. I should have worn something comfortable. But it was too late now.

Finally, the receptionist came trotting back. "This is Mildred," she said.

I was buffaloed. The receptionist was standing there all alone. For a minute I thought one of her "little people" was invisible, and then I realized that, clanging slowly up the long corridor behind a walker, was an old, old woman who must be Mildred Hull (husband deceased, no children).

I didn't know whether to run down the hall and stop the poor old thing from making the tortuous trip all the way to the front desk or just to stand there and wait, trying not to stare.

"Mildred says she doesn't know you," said the receptionist as though to fill the time. "But some of our little people get confused."

Our little people? "No," I said. "No, she wouldn't have any way of knowing me."

"But wasn't your group here at Christmas, or was that some other—?"

"Uh, Mrs. Hull?" I double-stepped it down the hall toward the bent figure.

The white head twisted up, the arms leaning heavily on the metal frame. "Last time I checked," she said. "And you?"

"We—I'm Kate Hensen. I'm a Girl Scout." What were you supposed to say?

"Oh, I get it. I couldn't imagine why any young girl I never heard of was coming to see me. I'm a merit badge."

"No. Really."

"Let me be a merit badge, please. I don't think I'm up to being a good deed for the day."

I guess I just stood there with my mouth open.

"If it's any comfort, our uniforms were worse. Lots worse." I tried to smile.

"Well, if I can't get you a merit badge, what can I do for you?" she asked.

"Maybe we could sit down somewhere?"

"Sure. No stamina, you kids today. No stamina."

She clumped her way to the little sitting area near the front door. I followed her, my hands out ready to catch her if she stumbled. I hovered around while she heaved herself into a straight chair and then nodded at me to take the overstuffed one next to it.

"Tell me about yourself," the old woman said, after she had caught her breath from the trip down the hall. "I haven't seen a live child close-up for ages. What are you like?"

"Like? Me?"

"Yeah. What would you be doing for example if you hadn't been shamed into coming to visit some poor little old lady today?"

"I—What?"

"Oh, come on now Kathryn or Kitty or—?" "Kate. Everyone calls me Kate."

"Is that what you want to be called?"

"Well, yeah, I guess so."

"I like to call people what they want to be called." She lowered her voice and leaned toward me. "Stick there," she whispered, jerking her head toward the receptionist, "calls me Mildred. I hate it."

"Stick?"

"Yeah, shhhh. We call her that because she looks like those stick figures little kids draw. You know."

I giggled out loud. I couldn't help myself.

"All these young aides here call me Mildred, too. I hate it. No one in my life ever called me Mildred."

"What do you want to be called?"

"My friends used to call me Millie." She leaned toward me again. "Promise you won't tell?"

I nodded, even though I had no idea what I was promising.

"My older brother used to call me Mildew."

"Mildew?" I looked at the woman, trying to see a little girl with a brother who called her Mildew. It was hard to imagine.

"For years, I burst into tears every time he said it," she said. "Silly, huh?"

"My brother used to call me Spook," I said.

"Spook?"

"My birthday is on Halloween. I hated that nickname. My mom calls me Pumpkin sometimes, and I don't mind at all."

"It's the way she says it, right?" She was quiet for a minute. "Ralph was my brother's friend. I was seventeen when I met him, and let me tell you the minute I saw that man I knew I wanted to marry him. When my brother introduced me as his sister, 'Mildew,' I was ready to kill him." She shook her head. "You know what Ralph called me till the day he died? Dewy." She gave her head a little shake. "Dewy. I thought it was the most beautiful name a girl could ever have."

I stared at her face hidden by thick, smudged glasses, trying hard to see that teenage girl so crazy with love. Then I realized Mrs. Hull was staring back and I said quickly, "Would you like to play some cards?"

"Cards? Why would I want to play cards? I hate cards."

"The, uh—" How could you tell a person they were on a

list (husband deceased, no children)? "They—uh—told me you liked to play cards."

"I play cards. Sure. With people who can't make conversation. Why should I play with you?" She cocked her head. "I guess we scare kids, don't we, with our white heads and false teeth and all our handicaps and infirmities. Yeah, I guess that's it. We're like monsters, aren't we, to healthy children like you."

"No," I said, "really." But I felt a tingle as I said it.

"I thought we'd never see anyone under the age of fifty in here again after last Christmas."

"Last Christmas?"

"A bunch of kids—Girl Scouts, too. I remember the uniforms. They came in here all brave and shiny to give the poor old coots some holiday cheer—" She started to giggle. "You're not going to believer this—"

Try me.

"My roommate. She's a harmless old soul, but they woke her out of a sound sleep. And right in the middle of these little girls sweetly chirping away, she comes roaring out of the room screaming her head off. Those little green girls ran like Frankenstein himself was upon them." She started to laugh. "I'm sorry," she said, "it does seem mean to laugh, but it was the funniest sight we've had around here since Stick got her new hairdo. We'll never forget that night." She looked at me sharply. "You think we're cruel? Getting so much fun at the expense of those poor scared children?"

I shook my head. "Someday they will probably look back on it and laugh," I said.

"We take our fun where we can get it around here," she said, almost as if apologizing. "I really don't approve of making fun of people"—she jerked her head toward the receptionist—"With perhaps the one major exception. I used to say to my daughter, June, I'd say—"

Daughter?

"What's the matter? Oh. If I have a daughter, why am I here? Or why doesn't she come to see me? Is that it?"

"Well, they said—"

"She's dead."

What were you supposed to say to something like that? I opened my mouth, but there were no words.

"It was a long time ago. But it's hard, you know. No, of course you don't know. You're what? Ten? Eleven?"

"I was twelve on Halloween."

"I hope you never know. I thought when Ralph died I would never get over it, but losing your child—having your beautiful child die—why should I be the one to live on and on?" she asked angrily. "What is my life worth? It isn't right," she said more quietly. "It's just not right." She fumbled around in the sleeve of the old housedress she was wearing. "Excuse me," she said. "This is embarrassing, but when I left my room, I didn't seem to bring a tissue."

I rooted in my pocket and pulled out a very wrinkled Kleenex. Mrs. Hull took off the thick glasses and wiped her eyes. "Thank you," she said. "You can mention that for the merit badge. Always be prepared. Or something like that. Don't tell them it was used. They may take off points."

"We don't suppose we have anything to report about our project at Logan Manor?" Bushey looked wistful, like a kid asking Santa for a toy that she knew she wasn't going to get.

"I went Sunday afternoon," I said. The rest of the troop

turned in their chairs to stare, but Bushey was smiling. She had a nice smile. She ought to smile more often.

"Yeah, I went through the list and picked a person they said didn't have any regular visitors. I didn't want to be running competition to somebody's darling grandchild."

"Did you get—you know who?" Laura whispered loudly. "Who?" asked Bushey.

"This woman we met when we were caroling last year. No," I said to the others, "I was pretty careful about that." They laughed nervously. "And?"

"Her name was Mrs. Hull and she said she didn't want to be my merit badge"—I ignored the noises the others were making—"but that she'd rather be a merit badge than a good deed."

"Which was she?" Amy asked.

"Neither. I liked her. I think she likes me, too. I'm going back to see her next week."

But Tuesday night Bushey called. The receptionist had made a mistake. Unaccompanied minors were not allowed to visit residents. "We could go with you," Bushey said.

"No!" As soon as I yelled it, I was sorry. "It's not you, Mrs. Bushey, it's the principle of the thing. I'm not going to misbehave. And I'm not going to give her some disease. I just want to talk with her. It wouldn't be the same with another person listening over our shoulders."

"If you're not comfortable with us, your mother might—"

"No, Mrs. Bushey, it's not you, really. I don't want my mother, either. I don't want to have to be baby-sat while I'm visiting with a friend."

"We understand," Bushey said, "and we think you're absolutely right. We will call the owner."

"Thanks, Bushey," I said, not even realizing that I'd

forgotten the "Mrs.," "but I think Mrs. Hull and I can handle this."

"May we say how proud we are, Scout Hensen?"

"Sure," I said.

I called Logan Manor immediately, but the night person told me that it was too late for calls. "It's only eight," I said.

"Our little people need their rest." Apparently the night person was a Stick clone.

The next afternoon, they let me talk to Mrs. Hull who was, as I was sure she would be, outraged.

"You come over here and we'll give that Mervin Wertz a piece of your mind. At my age, I don't have any to spare. And *don't* wear your uniform. Wear something that fits and makes you look like your parents could buy this place out and have money left over to burn."

When I arrived, dressed in the suit that my grandmother had sent me for Easter, Stick was on duty. I even wore my only pair of panty hose. I had started to sneak some of Mom's makeup, but I was afraid she'd make a fuss.

"Oh, yes, Kathy, isn't it?" Stick was rigid (pun intended).

"Kate Hensen. I think Mrs. Hull made an appointment for the two of us to speak to Mr. Wertz."

"Mildred and Gracie are already in his office," she said.

I opened the door. A man, a shriveled little man, was seated behind an enormous desk. Standing in front of him was Mrs. Hull, leaning on her walker with one hand and pounding on the desk with the other. In a chair on the opposite side of the room sat the person who Stick called Gracie, better known to me as "Stop-the-Noise." My blood froze, but I went on into the room.

Mrs. Hull was saying something that ended with " . . . the Constitution of the United States of America."

Mr. Wertz was getting very small and very pale. Everyone turned to look at me. I was glad I'd dressed so carefully.

"Is this the child?" Mr. Wertz asked.

"She has a name!" Mrs. Hull shouted. "She has a name. She is a person!"

"Kate Hensen," I said. "How do you do, Mr. Wertz?" I walked over and offered him my hand. I was so polite my grandmother would have fainted with joy.

Mr. Wertz ignored my hand. "It's very sweet of you little girls to want to cheer up our residents" (at least he didn't say "little people"), "but this is a medical and nursing facility, not a day care center." He smiled. I guess he thought it was a little joke. "We have some residents"—he gave Gracie a nervous glance—"who may be upset by unsupervised young visitors. And well, sometimes children are upset by elderly residents who, well, how shall I put it—?"

"Shut up!" Stop-the-Noise had jumped to her feet.

"As you see—"

"Shut up, I said!"

Mr. Wertz blinked rapidly. "Well, I don't really feel that we need to discuss this further. Our Gracie—"

"I'm not your Gracie!"

Mr. Wertz must have rung a bell or something because a young woman in a white uniform was there almost immediately. She took Gracie, or whatever Mrs. Hull's roommate was really named, by the arm and led her out of the room, shutting the door behind them. I could hear the old woman shouting down the hall as she went.

"You see, my dear, little children"—again my grandmother would have been proud that I didn't correct him—"sometimes, without even meaning to, can have an upsetting effect."

"Mr. Wertz, excuse me, but I think she was upset by you, not by me."

"She's right," Mrs. Hull said. "Mrs. Thompson hates being called Gracie."

"We always call our people by their first names," Mr. Wertz said.

"I know," said Mrs. Hull, "and some of us always hate it." I left that one alone. "Mr. Wertz," I said, "Mrs. Hull and I are friends—not close friends, I admit. We haven't had time for that. But we'd like to get to know each other better. We can't do that with chaperons. Frankly, we find the idea insulting. We are both perfectly intelligent people. I promise you that if you will allow me to come and visit Mrs. Hull, you will not regret it." I tried to put into my voice a hint that my family had untold millions, some of which would surely be donated to his nursing home if he agreed, but I can't be sure all that came through.

"And if it's any comfort to you, Mr. Wertz," said Mrs. Hull, "I will try to behave just as beautifully as my friend here."

"Whew," she said as we escaped after our triumph to a private corner of the lounge. "That was a near thing."

"Yeah," I said. "What's-her-name, Gracie, I mean—"

"Mrs. Thompson to you," Mrs. Hull said. "Yeah, great, wasn't she?"

"What?"

"Yeah, right on cue. We couldn't have done it without her. Remind me to pick up a Hershey bar for her. Kind of our merit badge system. You know how it goes."

"I'm learning," I said.

Bushey and I dragged the whole troop over to Logan Manor at Christmastime. Not to carol. Mrs. Hull vetoed that. We had a sing with the residents. Bushey, to my amazement, plays a mean piano, and Stick, when she unbends a bit, has a nice alto voice. She and I passed out songbooks, and the Girl Scouts scattered among the crowd. Gracie, Mrs. Thompson, I mean, mostly listened quietly, but when we got to "Joy to the World," I could hear her off-key "repeat the sounding joy" over and over long after the rest of us had gone on to the third verse. I smiled at Mrs. Hull, who smiled at me, and then Stick, who smiled at both of us. We all smiled at Bushey, who had a smile as wide as the stripes on the flag. We were all joyful. I think it was the first time I really understood the meaning of the word.

Guests

Whenever Pastor Nagai thought of his wife, he remembered the day last summer when she had taken her silk wedding kimono from the trunk and sold it for two tomatoes. The children had been so hungry. But the children were not hungry now. They would never be hungry again—nor full nor sad nor happy—nor alive.

With a crash of fire the tiny house had exploded, and they were all gone—his wife, his son, and the baby girl. One of her tiny sandals had been found in front of the greengrocer's nearly two blocks away.

Even as he had tried to fight his way into the burning wreckage of his home, he had heard a voice cry out: "Oh, pastor, where is your foreign god that he did not protect you from the American bombers? Is he asleep?"

"Perhaps"—another voice had joined the jeering—"he thinks all Japanese look alike!"

His heart's pain had soon blocked out the sound of the laughter. A few years before, these people who had been his neighbors had smiled and bowed politely to him on the street. Now he had become their enemy, a traitor to his native land, because he preached of the Americans' god. So great was their hatred that even the death of his family failed to draw from them a drop of human compassion.

His friend, Pastor Tanaka, had bicycled the twenty miles from Kawajima to hold the service at which Pastor Nagai was the only mourner. One could hardly count the policeman who had stood at the back with his arms crossed until Tanaka had mentioned "the Kingdom of God," at which he had whipped a small notebook from his pocket and proceeded to take notes.

Pastor Nagai was so alone. For a while he had tried to keep on having Sunday services. For two years they had been held at midnight and in secret so that the police would not harass the little congregation, for at first a few believers had continued to come. But, one by one, they had dropped away until only he and his wife and the sleeping children were there for the whispered hymns and prayers.

Now only he was left. He tried to pray a little each day and to read the scriptures, but he found himself turning again and again to the Psalms of anguish:

I am stricken, withered like grass
I cannot find the strength to eat.
Wasted away, I groan aloud
And my skin hangs on my bones. . . .
My enemies insult me all the day long;
Mad with rage they conspire against me.

I have eaten ashes for bread
And mingled tears with my drink.
In thy wrath and fury
thou hast taken me and flung me aside. . . .
My God, my God, why hast thou forsaken me?

Winter came, and nothing changed except the weather, which was cruel. He had moved into a corner of the tiny sanctuary, since the house had been destroyed, and there with whatever rags he could find stuffed about the windows, he tried to keep from freezing, huddled over a smoky charcoal burner. People died from such fumes, he knew—and sometimes hoped.

And then suddenly one day it was Christmas Eve. He had not remembered it, but, passing a shop window, he had seen a calendar with a large 24 printed in bright pink. His first thought was of his dead children, who had never known a Christmas without war. And then he thought of the year before, when his wife had tried so hard to find a merchant who would sell her a little rice for their Christmas dinner.

She had had a silk brocade sash, which had been in her family for three generations, that she would gladly have traded for a cup, even half a cup of rice, but the police had warned the merchants not to sell food to the traitors of Japan, so she had come home empty-handed.

Afterward, he himself had walked five miles into the country, which is a long journey on an empty stomach, to see a farmer who was a Christian and whose son the pastor had once helped prepare for his university entrance exams. The kind man had shared the last of his own grain, refusing to accept the sash in exchange. "You'll need it another day," he said.

How happy they had been last Christmas! Real rice, and almost enough of it to stop the constant pains in their empty bellies.

As he boiled the roots that were to be his meager meal, the memories of last Christmas, the farmer's generosity, and his family's joy shook loose the tentacles of his self-pity. From the closet he scrounged the stubs of some ancient Christmas candles. He would light them and have a proper service. To the devil with the police!

That afternoon he planned the hymns, even wrote a sermon, as though he were expecting fifty people to crowd into the little church, when, in fact, he expected no one at all. But it would be a proper service, and maybe his wife in heaven would know that he remembered her and for her sake had tried to worship the Infant King.

At ten he lit his seven stubby candles and seated himself at the wheezing pump organ.

Joy to the world! The Lord is come: Let earth receive her King. . . .

He sang at the top of his voice, daring that slick-booted young policeman who had burned up his volumes of Karl Barth to march in and arrest him. He almost prayed for the man to come. Why should he care if he were thrown into jail? What was this building, this town, to him but a jail?

Let every heart prepare him room, And heaven and nature sing.

He sang through all the verses and was tempted to repeat them, but as this was to be a proper service, he slid off the organ bench and stood behind the wooden pulpit. He bowed his head and closed his eyes.

"Let us pray."

"Oh, don't stop the music!"

The pastor's eyes popped open. In the doorway stood a little girl. About seven, he guessed, through he was seldom able to guess accurately, since his son had been only three when he died. Even in the dim candlelight he could see that she was dressed in rags, and he recognized her as a Korean child. The government had brought over laborers from Korea a few years before and impressed them into service for the war effort. They were housed in shacks on the other side of town.

"Would you like to come in for the meeting?" he asked gently.

She nodded, and slipping off her straw sandals, she climbed up into the room, her hands behind her back. She slid onto the floor before him and looked up expectantly.

He went on with the prayer, but he made it a short one. Children wiggled so terribly during long prayers, he remembered.

He inserted several more carols than he had planned, because the congregation obviously enjoyed the music most of all, and he skipped the offering entirely as most probably unnecessary.

Then there was the sermon. The careful notes, based on Jeremiah and on his memory of Karl Barth, were tucked into the back of his hymn book. He leaned over the pulpit and looked into the child's face. Her eyes were shining in the candlelight, as was her nose. Did all the children whom Jesus took on his knee have runny noses? He was tempted to offer her his handkerchief, ragged as it was, but he was afraid to offend her.

"Do you know about Jesus?"

She shook her head.

"Do you know, then, that there is one God who made the world and all of us in it?"

She shook her head again. And so the pastor began with Genesis and told her the story of God and man until he came to the time when God became man at Bethlehem.

"In a cave?" she asked. "Just like the cave we hide in when the bombers come?"

"Yes," he replied, "except there were no bombers then. They used the cave as a house for farm animals. Like a barn."

But she had never seen a barn. "If there were no bombers, was there no war in that country?"

"No war. That was over, but the great empire of Rome had won the war and conquered the tiny country, so there were many soldiers about."

"And secret police who beat you when you speak Korean in front of them?"

"Yes, secret police, I'm sure."

"And what did the new king do? Did he kill all the wicked soldiers and police?"

"No, he wasn't that kind of king."

The child was puzzled. Kings and emperors and presidents had power to crush and destroy in the world she knew. Surely a king . . . ?

"No. He went about helping people. If they were sick, he made them well." "Did he give them money and food?"

"Sometimes food. He didn't have any money."

"Then what happened?"

"He died. That is, he was killed. The soldiers and

leaders and a lot of the people hated him, and they had him killed."

"Why should they hate him?"

"I'm not completely sure. Perhaps they were afraid of his goodness. Perhaps they thought he was a traitor. Or perhaps they resented the way he loved the poor and the unhappy people."

"Did he love Koreans and Christ lovers, too?"

"Yes." The pastor smiled. "Even those."

"Is that all the story?"

"Oh, no. If that were the end of the story, we would be hopeless. Our King would be dead." And as the pastor told of how the king had died and then risen, some light dawned in his own dark spirit. "He is alive. Right here with us. But we can't see him."

"Yes, we can," the child said. "You look like the king." She got up and padded barefoot to him, and as she did so, she took her hand from behind her back and held out to him a roasted sweet potato. How had he missed the smell earlier? It came to his nostrils now like the sweet manna of the wilderness. The two of them sat down together while he carefully divided the treasure—she must have stolen it—and ate it slowly together.

He hated for the evening to end, but he knew it must be very late. The night watchman calling the hour before midnight had passed by some time ago. At first she protested, but at last consented to go when he promised more music and stories another day.

He bade her good night and began to extinguish the candles, which were now nothing but wicks swimming in puddles of wax.

"Uncle."

He looked up to see the child in the doorway. And behind her, standing half-hidden in the shadows, was the figure of a man. He knew without seeing the face that it was the shiny-booted policeman who had confiscated his bicycle, burned his books, and taken notes at his wife's funeral. A thrill of fear went through him. How long had the policeman been standing there? What had he heard? Lord, what had he said in that crazy sermon? But he did not want the child to see his fear, so he said simply: "Come back in, little one, and bring your friend in with you."

"I found him waiting outside the door," she explained. "Perhaps he liked the music, too."

The policeman stepped up into the church without bothering to remove his boots. The pastor pretended not to notice. "My son," he said, "the service was just ending, but since you've taken such trouble to come, perhaps you would like for us to continue it a little longer?"

The younger man's lips curled for a sarcastic reply, but the pastor did not wait for it.

"If you'll just sit there in the front with the child. . . ." He looked straight into the proud face. To Pastor Nagai's surprise he found it to be a young face. The eyes above the sneering mouth shifted slightly under the pastor's gaze. It is only a child, the pastor realized, another child who has never heard the story.

He took his place behind the pulpit and opened the Bible. There was only moonlight now, too dark for him to read by, but he knew the passage by heart.

"And it came to pass in those days there went out a decree from Caesar Augustus that all the world should be taxed. . . ." The policeman took out a notebook and began to write.

"And, lo, the angel of the Lord came upon them, and the glory of the Lord shone round about them: and they were sore afraid. And the angel said unto them, Fear not. . . ." For the first time in many years, Pastor Nagai obeyed the angel's word.

Watchman, Tell Us of the Night

I volunteered to work Christmas Eve because I was trying to put off going home. I mean, who wants to go home empty-handed at Christmastime? My wife would understand. She wasn't expecting anything. Fact was, she'd have been upset if I'd spent money for anything but food. Ever heard of a hungry farmer?

Well, okay, I'm not a farmer anymore. My father was, and his father before him. They left me their land and their dreams, and I lost it all. If only I hadn't bought the fancy new tractor, if only it had rained, if only I had planted soy instead of wheat, if only . . .

A bunch of if onlys and my house and land—my granddaddy's house and land—are auctioned off for a quarter of what they're worth. My wife and two little girls are in a run-down city walk-up. Sheila's six and Michelle is only four. I think what hurts as much as anything is that in a few years they won't even remember the farm—the green and gold of the fields, the old splintery wood barn that smells so sweet with hay, the baaing of the sheep and the jangling of their bells as they come back to the fold at sunset.

But, hey, I'm lucky—I got a job. Night watchman at Friedman's department store at the Pine Crest mall. I got me a blue uniform and a cap like a navy officer; a big flashlight, size of a baseball bat, on my belt; and this big holster with a pistol snug in the genuine leather. Lord forbid I ever have to use it. Like my daddy said, I couldn't hit the side of a barn with an M-16. He gave up taking me deer hunting by the time I was fifteen. I was hopeless, he said. Couldn't do nothing right. I'd probably end up shooting the game warden or something.

My Sheila, when she saw me all dressed up in my uniform, she told me I look just like a movie star. My wife burst out crying. I'm just glad my mother never lived to see this day. Or my dad. He'd never forgive me for losing his land. He hardly forgave me for being his kid in the first place.

But, hey, that's not the story I'm going to tell you. It's coming up Christmas, see, and nobody wants to work Christmas Eve. So the boss offers overtime for a six-to-six shift. I jump at it. I ain't got nothing but candy and two dollar-ninety-nine-cent stuffed bears to put in the kids' stockings anyway. If I work hard, maybe next year—who knows?

They close the store at six o'clock on Christmas Eve. By eight, when I look out the front door, the parking lot's almost empty, 'cept way to the north end where the all-night Peoples is sucking in a bunch of last-minute shoppers. I get so lonesome seeing all that empty asphalt, I just go back to the lounge, pour myself a cup of coffee, and turn

on the radio. They're playing Christmas music. I nearly flip
the dial. I mean, I'm not big on Christmas this year. But it
isn't "Santa Claus is coming to town" they're playing. It's
mostly carols. Hey, I tell myself, that's what Christmas is all
about—Jesus being born in a barn—and it wasn't one that
belonged to his daddy, either.

I don't want you to think I blame God or anything. Heck.
It was probably all my fault. If I'd been smarter . . . My dad
always said I was too dumb to milk a cow with both hands
at the same time. But to tell you the truth, I'm not too big
on God this year, either. I prayed. I really prayed. I couldn't
believe God meant for me to lose that land. It was kind of a
trust from my granddaddy, and he was a real fine Christian.
He went to church three times a week and made his kids
swear never to smoke or drink. My daddy never did, either.
He was a deacon. When he died, there was standing room
only in the church.

I used to go to that same church. Not every Sunday. Not
easy for a farmer to get away every week. But my wife always
went—took the kids to Sunday school and everything. When
things started getting tight, she told me I should pray more.
So I tried. I really did. First I prayed it would rain. It didn't.
Not hardly for two years. Then I prayed the John Deere guy
would buy back for the tractor for at least half of what I'd
paid. He wouldn't. Then I prayed the price of wheat would
go up. It fell out the bottom. Finally, I gave up praying for
piddling little things. Hey, I said, forget the little stuff, just
gimme a doggoned miracle.

So here I am. I've made my hourly rounds and it's
about three o'clock in the morning. I'm listening to "While
Shepherds Watched Their Flocks by Night" and thinking
about how the first thing I had to sell off was my sheep.

I loved those stupid sheep. My daddy wouldn't ever keep sheep. Too dumb for him. But maybe I wanted something around that made me feel smart. I'd look in the face of some old ewe, and she'd give me this worshiping look like she'd trust me with her whole silly life. I guess it's why some people keep dogs. Me, I like sheep. Yeah, I'd go for a miracle—one that would give me back enough land to keep a few sheep. How 'bout it, God?

There I was leaning back, my feet up on the table where the coffeemaker sits, my eyes closed, when I hear this noise. Or think I do. I slam my legs down, barely missing Mr. Coffee, and shut off the radio at the same time. And I just listen. There's a lot a noises in a big empty store at night, the heating system for one. The first night I was on duty I might have shot a heating duct in the heart if I hadn't caught myself in time—and if I had been able to shoot straight. My hand was shaking like an aspen in a gale wind.

Well, I sit there and listen to the heat go on and off—*ping*—and carry on. The wind is blowing the flaps of the vent in the ladies' room, and there's a couple of other squawks and groans that I'd never located but what I know by now are just part of the scenery. I don't hear them ordinary sounds anymore. I just hear the sound of my own breathing, which is hard and fast.

Then, I hear it again. It's faint and far away—must be at the back of the building. Weird sound. Only thing I can figure it sounds like is some lamb out on the hillside bawling for its momma.

I shake my head to make sure it ain't cobwebbed and start out in the direction of the noise. There's lights on in the store, but they're low and kinda spooky. I'm sweating some. *Pull your gun. Don't walk toward any strange sound with your gun in the holster. You won't have time later.* Those were my instructions during my training. Training. Hah. Less than half a day. Then a couple of nights with another guard and I'm on my own.

I pull the gun out. I can still hear the sound. It's coming from the loading area, where crates are piled. Anybody could hide, drill me through the ticker, and I'd never know what hit me. I'm sweating so much now I have to stop, take off my hat, and wipe my face so I can see to walk through the door to the loading area.

Probably a cat. There're plenty of them behind the A & P, digging in the garbage. All we got behind Friedman's is empty cartons from the floor models, but how's a cat to know. A new cat on the block would have to nose around a bit, wouldn't he, 'fore he could find the garbage with the goodies?

I push the door out gentle and then sneak through, gun in one hand, flashlight in the other, and *boom!* I'm sprawled on the dock. My flashlight goes one way and the stupid gun the other. It don't go off. I forgot to release the safety.

Anyhow, I yell, "Who's there?" and this box under my legs starts to squawl. Well, I figure whatever's in there ain't gonna shoot me, unless it's some delinquent midget, but I can't hardly stop shaking. Finally, I get up, get my flashlight and gun, put the gun back in the holster, and shine the light into this Zenith DVD carton—right into the pinched-up, bright red face of this baby. Yeah, baby. I mean little baby—hardly more'n month or two old from the size.

"Hey, you!" I yell at the refrigerator cartons. "You come back here and get this kid!" The refrigerator cartons don't answer. Or the stove boxes or the dishwasher crates, either. "I mean it!" I yell, shining the beam all around. "You can't just walk off and leave your kid like this. It's against the law! I wasn't sure about that, but if it ain't against the law, it oughtta be, right?

I keep yelling and watching for some sign of life rustling through the boxes, but it's still as the cover of the moon. Except for this kid, who by this time is squawling and shaking the box so hard the Zenith looks like real lightning. I give up and take the box inside. It's cold as Hades on the loading dock. Shouldn't leave a baby out there. Shouldn't leave a baby at all.

On TV, when somebody leaves a kid on the doorstep, there's always a note. Well, poking around in the box, I don't come up with a note, but I do find a bottle, less than half full, plus one extra Pampers. Not what you'd call long-range planning, but enough, maybe to get me through till six.

First, I change the kid, and it's a boy. I never fussed about not having a boy. My girls are the sweetest little things you ever saw. I'm kind of a hero to them. And, well, I remember— my daddy and his daddy, my daddy and me. Maybe the men in my family don't do so good with sons. But here was this little guy churning his legs like a fullback and yelling his ugly little head off. I could feel something in my throat the size of a baseball.

The bottle is icy cold, as you could guess. I take off the nipple and warm the milk for a few seconds in the microwave. Then I test it on my wrist. Hey, you think I don't know how to do this stuff? I'm a pro. Two kids of my own and a small army of bottle-fed lambs, if you add them up over the years.

Okay, so you're wondering why I don't call the cops. I could give you lots of reasons, but none of 'um would be true. I don't call the cops because it never once occurs to me. I guess something was niggling at me, though. Else why do I smuggle the kid in a shopping bag past Gus when he comes to relieve me at six? It's my secret. I don't want to have to explain it to Gus.

I get home. Usually I'm dog tired climbing those four flights to the apartment. This morning I just bounce up, baby and all. There're no lights on when I open the door. When I was a kid we used to get up in the middle of the night to see what Santa brought. I guess it's different for my girls. They've learned not to expect much.

We still got cloth diapers from when Michelle was a baby. I change the kid and wrap it in an old baby blanket and tiptoe into the bedroom, where I put it down on the bed beside Pauline.

"What time is it?" Pauline always wants to know the time. I kid her. The Day of Judgment, the trumpet will be blowing and Pauline will be asking Gabriel, "What time is it?"

"Merry Christmas," I say. "Look what I brought you."

Then she turns and sees the baby and her eyes get wide as old satellite dishes.

"What in the . . .?"

"I was praying for a miracle," I say, "and here comes this baby."

She makes me explain, so I do, and then she says, "Why didn't you call the police?"

I don't want to tell her I never thought about it until that minute, so I say, "Why? The kid ain't done nothing wrong."

"You know what I mean." Pauline is the type that's very practical. And then, real soft, 'cause she's cuddling him and looking into his little pinched face: "We can't feed another kid, Gary. You know that."

I'm starting to try to figure out an answer, but the girls come running in. They see Pauline holding the baby, and

Michelle is ready to explode she's so excited. "Baby Jesus! Baby Jesus! Sheila, Sheila, look! I told you Santa Claus was going to bring us something special!" Michelle hasn't got her various Christmas stories sorted out too good yet.

I look at Pauline and Pauline looks at me. Neither of us is gonna tell Michelle that somebody left this beautiful little ugly kid in a Zenith DVD carton behind Friedman's department store.

This is our private little miracle, isn't it? Oh, I'll run a personal in the paper and ask the party that left a package on the loading dock at Friedman's to call the party below to identify contents and claim, but that's the most I'm gonna do for now. I'll figure out how to feed him—how to make him legal. Maybe I'll even figure out how to be a better father to him than my dad was to me.

But all that will wait for another day. I go down the four flights of stairs and out into the empty street. I want to watch the sun come up in the sky on Christmas morning, and I feel—how can I say it? I feel close to what's all about for the first time in my life. Like I told Pauline, I prayed for a miracle, and God gave me a baby. Isn't that what He did that other time? Isn't that what all the cheering has been about all these years?

Why the Chimes Almost Rang

E llie had found the book in her grandmother's house last summer. She had read and reread it so many times that her grandmother told her she could take it home with her. There were eleven stories in the book, but the story she loved best was the first one. It was called "Why the Chimes Rang," and it was about a boy named Pedro and his little brother who lived in a land far away and a time long past.

The little boys lived out in the countryside and had never been to the city, but they had often heard of the magnificent church there and they were determined to go and see it for themselves. You see, there was a mystery about this church. It was not only enormous and beautiful, but it had a tower that stretched to the sky. People said that in the top of the tower there was a set of beautiful chimes, but that might have been only a rumor because no one alive had ever heard them ring. The story was that they would only ring on Christmas Eve when someone laid the perfect gift for the Christ child on the altar.

The boys wanted to see the great church and be a part of its wonderful Christmas Eve service. It was a long trip and it was dark before they reached the city, but just at the edge of the city the two brothers found a woman asleep in the snow and they knew, as any one who lives in a snowy climate knows, that if you go to sleep in the snow you'll probably never wake up. Pedro, even though it broke his heart to miss it all, sent his little brother ahead to the church to attend the service and then bring back help.

Well, at the end of the magnificent service, all the rich people went forward to leave their gold and silver and jewels as gifts to the Christ child. But no chimes rang. The king himself had come and he took off his crown and laid it on the altar, but still, no chimes. The disappointed congregation went on to sing the last hymn, when suddenly, the organist stopped playing, and in the silence everyone could hear, high up in the tower, the music of the chimes. But only those closest to the altar had seen the little boy put his big brother's coin on the altar.

Ellie loved the story. All fall she made her little brother act it out with her until he cried. Jake said he was tired of having to walk all the way to the back of the yard, climb up on the garden stool, and stand on tiptoe to put the nickel on the bird feeder. Why couldn't he stay beside the back door and pet the dog—who was happy to lie in the sun and be the freezing woman in the snow?

"Because I'm eight and you're only five," Ellie said. "It's the big brother who stays behind and rubs snow in the face of the dying woman, not the little brother."

"You're not a brother," Jake said. "You're a sister."

"The writer made a mistake," Ellie said. "It's always girls and ladies who take care of dying people in these situations, not boys. Besides, you're the one who gets to be right there when the chimes ring." With that she poked the wind chimes with a stick to set them tinkling.

Jake sighed. Ellie could see he was about to protest for the tenth time that the chimes were by the house, not by the bird feeder, but she gave him a look so he'd know there wasn't any use in protesting.

Winter came, and when it did, Ellie was overjoyed. Now they could play "Why the Chimes Rang" in real snow, but it didn't work out. The dog refused, for one thing, to lie in the snow for more than a couple of minutes at a time, and Jake took one trip to the bird feeder, claimed that the snow had gotten into his boots, and went indoors to request a restorative cup of hot chocolate from their mother. It didn't matter that he would go sledding for hours, getting soaked to the skin, without a murmur.

Ellie had sense enough to know that it didn't really matter. She and Jake had only been *playing* "Why the Chimes Rang." She didn't want it to be pretend. She wanted to do something so wonderful that church chimes would really ring.

Every Sunday when they went to church, she looked up at the stubby tower on top of their church. If only their church had a steeple like the Unitarian Church. It would be much more like the great church in the story. It might even have secret chimes at the top.

"Does our church have chimes?" she asked her mother.

"I think there is something on the organ that sounds like chimes."

"No, I mean, chimes in the tower."

Her mother laughed. "Oh, no, nothing that grand. We don't even have a bell in the tower."

But, thought Ellie, there might be secret chimes in the tower. Chimes that hadn't rung in the more than hundred years since the church had been built, so no one alive knew they were up there. They hadn't been heard because no one had given the perfect gift on Christmas Eve. That was it. So all she had to do was figure out the perfect gift and that would make the secret chimes ring out. Everyone would be astounded. "Who," they'd ask each other, "who made the chimes ring?" Maybe she'd never tell, but then it would be a shame if no one knew. Someone would figure out that it was Ellie McPherson and whisper it to someone else. She wouldn't say anything, but when asked, she might blush and then everyone would know and be impressed. It would be known forever after as the miracle of the chimes—the child in the church who with her perfect gift had made the mysterious, forgotten chimes ring out from the tower in the little green church.

It bothered her a bit that Pedro hadn't planned it at all. He and his little brother (who didn't have a name because he wasn't the hero like Pedro) had practically stumbled on the poor woman in the snow. There wasn't any chance of that kind of accident happening for her. Mom and Dad would drive the car to the parking lot beside the church and the walk would be shoveled and sprinkled with the melt ice stuff, and in the tiny yard between the walk and the building no one would be almost asleep in the snow waiting to be rescued.

It was a shame. If only they'd find someone lying there and she could say to her family: "Go on in. Don't miss the service. I'll stay here and rub snow in her face so she won't go to sleep and freeze. And here—" at this point she'd hand Jake her gift "—take this and put it in the offering plate for me." If her parents protested, she'd remind them that she would be perfectly safe right there under the streetlight just a few feet from the door. And oh, how lovely, outdoors, so near the tower, she'd be able to hear the chimes echoing out across the town.

She wouldn't even have to figure out the perfect gift, it could be like just a nickel or a dime, because her real present, her perfect present, would be taking care of the freezing woman. She heaved a great sigh. She knew perfectly well that it was only in a land far away and a time long ago that things like that could happen. If her Dad saw someone lying in the churchyard, he'd whip out his cell phone and call 911 faster than you could say "Jiminy Christmas," and the ambulance would be there almost before he put the phone back in his pocket.

Christmas Eve came and she still hadn't figured out the perfect gift. She'd saved part of her allowance all month in case she thought of something. She almost spent it for mittens for the mitten tree, but half the church had bought mittens for poor kids, so her adding a pair was not going to look like some special present—a present that would make the chimes ring. She thought about buying a huge can of beef stew for the food closet, but people had been bringing in canned goods all year to give to the needy—there was nothing special about one more can of stew. The homeless shelter wanted toothbrushes for the people who were staying there. She thought about using her money to get a really nice toothbrush *and* a large tube of toothpaste, but her Mom went out while she was at school and bought six toothbrushes and six tubes of toothpaste. One of each would look just plain puny.

So she started for church with her saved allowance in her pocket. It wouldn't be much of anything in the way of a present—eight quarters—not enough to make a doorbell chime, but time had run out and she didn't have a real present.

There was plenty of snow in the churchyard. She stopped on the walk just to make sure no one was lying there. Maybe there was a funny bump there beside the bushes . . .

"Come on, Ellie, sweetie, we don't want to miss the prelude."

There was nothing to do but follow her family in.

She usually loved the carols. The first one was "O Come, All Ye Faithful." She's known most of the words since she was six, but she didn't feel very faithful tonight. She'd wanted to do something really great, and God just hadn't let her. She rattled the quarters in her pocket. Her mother put her hand gently on Ellie's pocket and formed a "Shh" with her lips.

The choir began to sing a song about the deep mid-winter which made Ellie think of the story and how much she had wanted it to come true and how it wasn't going to. And then she heard the words the choir was singing "what shall I give him, poor as I am? If I were a shepherd I would give a lamb. If I were a wise man, I would do my part. But what can I give him—give my heart."

Just like that—like giving your heart was some kind of great gift. You say you give your heart, there isn't some big hole left. You still got a heart beating away inside. Phooey. That's what she thought.

She glanced at the program. The offering was next and she wasn't giving up half of four weeks allowance for nothing. She whispered to her mother, "I gotta go to the bathroom," and slipped out of the pew, down the aisle, through the vestibule and over to the stairs.

She heard the racket before she turned the corner at the bottom of the stairs. It was a woman going through the shelves where Miss Sylvia and the deacons kept the food for the needy. The stranger had a backpack beside her on the floor and she was handing cans to a little boy who was stuffing them into the backpack.

"What are you doing?" The words just popped out of Ellie's mouth.

The woman turned around and stared at her. "I'm getting me and the boy here something to eat," she said and turned back toward the closet.

"But . . ."

"Well, that's about all I can carry anyway," the woman said.

The little boy began to whimper. "Shut up," she said. "We'll eat when we get back. Can't eat cans like a goat." She smiled at Ellie. It was supposed to be funny, but the boy started to cry.

"Got anything to eat in the kitchen?" she asked Ellie. "He don't think he can wait."

"I'm not in charge . . ." Ellie began, trying to remember where Miss Sylvia had been sitting. Oh fudge, she was in the choir loft. Ellie needed a grown-up. But the woman was already walking across the vestry and was headed for the kitchen. There was nothing for Ellie to do but follow her. The woman was crashing around in the dark. "Where are the damn lights?" she yelled. Maybe Miss Barbara or Miss Pam or someone upstairs would hear and come running down. The woman was nothing but a thief—on Christmas Eve, too. She must have known everyone would be upstairs singing and carrying on and she could just help herself to whatever she wanted. Ellie wondered if there was anything really valuable in the kitchen

"Never mind. I got it." The lights went on overhead and then in the refrigerator.

"Ice cream!" the little boy screamed. Surely Mr. Mike who was ushering would hear him, but they were singing "Joy to the World" and that was always a loud one.

"Got spoons around here?"

Ellie nodded dumbly. It took her three tries but she found the silver drawer and handed the woman a couple of spoons.

"Care to join us?"

Ellie just looked at the woman. Since she, Ellie, belonged it might not be actual stealing for her to eat the church's ice cream, but it didn't seem right. The woman hadn't waited for an answer. The two intruders just stood there in the kitchen and ate the ice cream right out of the carton. It was nearly a whole half gallon of the strawberry, chocolate, and vanilla striped kind—her favorite, too. But she certainly wasn't going to eat any. It wasn't honest and it wasn't sanitary either. Her mother would be horrified. Upstairs it was quiet except for the rumble of the preacher's voice. She was missing the story. She really liked the stories he told on Christmas Eve.

"Had enough?" the woman asked. The boy nodded, but he didn't stop. He just ate faster, dropping globs of ice cream on the front of his already dirty little jacket. The woman opened the refrigerator again and took out a pound of butter. She shoved it into her backpack.

"Come on, Junior. You can have more to eat when we get home." She picked up the backpack and slung it over her shoulder. "Hey, whatcha got there?"

"What?"

"In your pocket." She came over to the counter where Ellie was standing. "You was jiggling something."

Ellie shook her head. "I—"

"Come on. You got plenty and I bet tonight Santa Claus is gonna load you up. The kid here could do with something beside canned soup in his stocking, right? Come on, be a sport."

What could she do? She took the quarters out and laid them on the counter.

"That's all you got?"

Ellie nodded.

"Well, keep it. It won't buy nothing much and we wouldn't want to take your last quarter, would we Junior?" She started out of the kitchen, leaving the boy behind staring at the money. Except for the tracks his tears had left, his face was filthy and his hands sticking out of the too short sleeves of his jacket were chapped and raw.

She wasn't sure what made her do it, but Ellie scooped up the quarters and stuffed them into the little boy's pocket. "Merry Christmas," she whispered.

His eyes widened and then clutching his pocket to keep his treasure safe, he ran to catch up with his mother.

Ellie heard the quiet strains of "Silent Night" coming from upstairs. That meant the service was almost over. Quickly she rinsed the dirty spoons at the sink. Ellie threw the almost empty ice cream carton in the trash and turned off the kitchen light. She crept up the dark staircase and when she came into the vestibule Mr. Mike was dimming all the overhead lights so that the only light in the sanctuary was from the large candles up front and in the windows and the dozens of tiny flames from all the little candles being held by the congregation. It was so beautiful, it made Ellie catch her breath.

Mr. Mike handed her a lighted candle, and Ellie realized that Miss Alison had stopped playing the organ and the congregation was almost whispering the words:

With the angels let us sing
Alleluia to our King:
Christ the Savior is born,
Christ the Savior is born.

A shiver went down her spine. It was almost like hearing the chimes ring.

Broken Windows

There was something dreadfully wrong with the Sunday sermon, but Philip, for all his thirty-five years in the pulpit ministry and ten years as senior pastor of prestigious First Church, couldn't put his finger on the trouble. He was sure that if he asked his wife, she would say it was the text. Grace was always generous with constructive criticism. "It's a text for Lent," she would say. On the other hand, Mike, his assistant until last month, would have congratulated Philip on the text, while secretly laughing at him for choosing it. Mike was one of those young men determined to out-Christian the Bible. It was always good for a wealthy downtown church to have a social radical like Mike around, but—Philip sighed despite himself— something of a relief when he went on to become someone else's noisy conscience.

The text in question was Psalm 51, verse 17: "The sacrifices of God are a broken spirit; a broken and a contrite heart, O God, thou wilt not despise." The older members of the congregation did love to hear the King James, but perhaps it would help him now also to read it in the Revised Standard Version. "The sacrifice acceptable to God," read the RSV, "is a broken spirit; a broken and contrite heart, O God, thou wilt not despise."

Grace would say it was a strange choice for the Sunday before Christmas, but he wouldn't tell her ahead of time. It was better that way. The problem, he knew, was not with the text. It exactly fitted the Christmas story: Zacharias and Elizabeth, Joseph and Mary, the humble shepherds, even the kings of the East—broken and contrite spirits offered up to God. So why wasn't it working? Why was the taste of the words like Shredded Wheat without milk?

He got up, the sermon in his hand, and began to pace the study. Perhaps if he read it aloud: "When Zacharias entered the sanctuary that day to offer up the incense—"

Crash! He ducked instinctively, which was a good thing because he could feel the baseball brush his hair as it flew over. It was stopped by the plaque from the Rotary Club commemorating his presidency. Philip paused only long enough to pick up the ball and then raced out the door.

By the time he got around to the patch of lawn, the children were long gone, of course. The damp grass was full of their damaging footprints, and above, the jagged glass of the study window sparkled in the late afternoon sun.

He allowed himself the luxury of a curse. How many times had he chased children off the last square of grass left to the church? And now the window. There was no one he could get to fix it on a Saturday afternoon, and with

Christmas so near, there was probably no way of getting it repaired for a week or more. He was about to return to his study when he realized that the little vandals had left something behind. He walked over to investigate.

Philip picked the object up and immediately regretted doing so. The thing was filthy and gave off a distinct odor. One paw was gone and another going, but Philip could tell that at one time it had passed for a bear. When his own children had been young, they had teddy bears. Becky had slept with one of the silly things for years.

"'At's my brother's bear," a voice said. Philip looked down into a dirt-streaked face. The boy was about nine or ten; although since his own children were grown, he had trouble guessing ages.

"'At's my brother's bear," the boy said again, sticking out a skinny arm.

"Just a minute," Philip said. "You're the very person I was looking for."

"Me?"

"Yes, you. What about that window, young man?"

"I don't know nothing about no window. I just come to get my brother's bear."

"Which he dropped while you were running away."

The boy's eyes flickered defensively. "I don't know about no window."

"Well, I think I'll just keep the bear and the baseball until you remember."

"What do you want with that stinking bear?"

Philip coughed. He was beginning to feel like a fine actor caught in a bad play. "You children," he said in a voice that a Shakespearean actor would have envied, "you children have repeatedly been asked *not* to play on the church lawn.

You've ruined what little grass there was, and now you've broken a window."

"I don't know nothing—"

"You said that before. But I should like to talk to your parents about who is to pay for this window you know nothing about."

The boy shrugged. "The preacher never said nothing about us playing here."

"Young man, *I* am the preacher."

"The other one."

He must mean Mike. Of course—Mike would have organized Little League on the church's patch of lawn given half a chance. "That preacher is no longer with us."

The boy snuffled, shifting his weight from foot to foot. Out of the side of his eye, Philip could see a small child half hidden behind the corner of the building. The owner of the bear, no doubt.

"If you want the bear," Philip said loudly, "bring your parents to see me in my office. It's the room," he added, lowering his head toward the boy's, "with the broken window." He straightened, turned, and strode inside, telling himself that the whole problem with the world these days was that children were never made to take responsibility for their actions. Later, as he taped a patch of plastic wrap over the hole, he wondered if he had done the right thing. It did seem small, keeping the little boy's toy, but then again . . .

He had gone back to the sermon, almost forgetting about the window, when the outside bell rang. He got up impatiently. All the church doors remained locked for security, and when there was no secretary here, it was worse than annoying to have to see who was at the door.

A woman was there with the two boys. "Oh," he said.

"Come in."

She hesitated. "Bobby says you got Wayne's bear." She sounded angry.

"Let's talk about it in the office, shall we?" He felt the need for time.

The woman sat perched on the edge of the chair he offered. The children stood close to her.

"The problem," Philip began, "is that the church lawn is really not a public park."

"The other reverend never cared," she said.

"Yes. Well, you see, there isn't enough room. And there are the windows. . . ."

"I don't have no money," she said. "My husband been out of work for weeks and now he's gone. I don't know where." She spoke sharply as though her misfortunes were somehow to be blamed on Philip. "The kids ain't going to have no Christmas as it is. They understand that. But they don't understand why Wayne can't have his bear. That's the meanest thing I ever heard of. Wayne's had that bear since before he could walk."

She looked Philip up and down. "Here's this five-year-old kid. His daddy's done took off just before Christmas. He ain't gonna have any Santa Claus. And this big preacher steals his teddy bear. I hope to God that makes you happy."

"Mrs.—Mrs.—I don't want his bear, for heaven's sake."

"Where's that other reverend? Lord, when we was in trouble before, he used to help us out, not steal. . . ."

"Mr. Coates has moved to another congregation."

"So? That figures." She stood up so abruptly that she nearly knocked the two boys over. "I guess you might as well say good-bye to your teddy bear, Wayne. I'm sure the reverend got better things to do than talk to us."

"Now look here, Mrs.—Mrs.—"

"You don't care what my name is!"

"If you'd give me a chance, I would. Just sit down, will you?"

Again she nearly knocked her sons over, but she did sit down.

Philip went over to his desk and got the bear. He took it to the smaller child. "I'm sorry I made you unhappy, Wayne. Here's your bear."

The boy looked at Philip as though he suspected some foul trick and then snatched the bear.

Philip sat down. "Now, Mrs.—"

"Slaytor," she said.

"Mrs. Slaytor. I—we—the church would like very much to know how we might help."

By the time they left, he had given Mrs. Slaytor money out of his own pocket to buy groceries, and as soon as they were gone, he called the head of the service committee and asked her about arranging for presents for the Slaytor's Christmas. "Oh," the woman laughed when he told her a rough outline of what had happened, "some of Mike's Miserables, eh?"

"Mike's what?"

"Mike's Miserables. He was always after us to help them. He had this little pep talk about the church caring for those who live in 'the shadow of her spire.' We called them Mike's Miserables. Not so poetic, but more descriptive. He had quite a little collection of them."

The Sunday before Christmas was always a wonderful day at First Church. Years before, someone had donated an almost life-sized crèche, which was placed in the left alcove of the huge sanctuary. The figures had been carved out of Philippine mahogany, and a church member had worked out a setting that made the Holy Family appear as though outlined within a cave. A light shone up from the manger into the face of the mother. In the right alcove stood a giant Christmas tree shimmering in white and silver. The choir loft was banked with red poinsettias, and the great candelabra were lit.

The Christmas Sunday sermon went well. Perhaps the little episode with the Slaytors had helped him, Philip thought. They had even come to church that morning, the three of them still looking a bit defiant. All in all, it was a wonderful service. He shook every hand that passed him at the back, and then started across the length of the sanctuary toward the robing room. Something about the crèche light caught his attention. Maybe the bulb was weak. He went over to investigate.

He saw at once that there was an object on top of the light. He could hardly believe his eyes. It was his nose that convinced him. Wayne Slaytor's bear was lying in the manger.

Philip didn't know whether to laugh or to cry. Why? Why? He had been glad to help the Slaytors out—the money—the arrangements—but now he had other things he must do. He tried to think of the bear as a little child's thank-you to God. It didn't work. The bear meant something else.

He took Grace home, got a hurried lunch, and drove back downtown. The bear was in a shopping bag, but its aroma filled the car. The black Lincoln Town Car suddenly seemed very long and very new as it pulled up in front of the dirty brick apartment house. He breathed a prayer and went in.

The Slaytors were on the fourth floor. He climbed the stairs slowly. At sixty he thought of himself as still vigorous, but even so four floors were a bit of exercise. The whole building smelled liked Wayne's bear.

Mrs. Slaytor answered his knock. "I—uh—seem to have Wayne's bear again," he said, holding out the bag.

"He tole me he left it at church."

"May I come in?"

"I guess." She stepped back. "Boys, turn off the TV. The reverend's here." They didn't obey, but they both turned to look at him.

"I brought back your bear, Wayne," Philip said, taking it out of the shopping bag and offering it to the child.

Wayne shrank back, shaking his head.

"Thank the reverend, Wayne."

Wayne just shook his head.

"He don't want it, Reverend," his brother said. "He give it to God."

"Lord, Wayne. God don't want that smelly old bear. Now thank the reverend." Philip went over and knelt down by the boy's stool. "What's the matter, Wayne?" The child's eyes filled with tears. He squeaked out something totally unintelligible.

Philip turned to Bobby. "What did he say?"

"He said he want his daddy."

"Oh."

"That's how come he give the bear to God. So as God would send back his daddy for Christmas."

"Lord, Wayne. You better leave God alone. He ain't got time for your foolishness. Ain't that right, Reverend?"

"Well . . ."

"See, Wayne? Reverend know all about God, and he knows God don't mess with people like us. Right, Reverend?"

"Well . . ."

"You just make God mad acting like that. See, the reverend knows I'm right. You can't bribe God with no teddy bear. Right, Reverend?"

"Yes, no!" The woman would drive him wild. He knelt as close to the now-weeping child as he could. "Listen, Wayne," he said softly. "God knows you love that bear, and he knows you love your daddy. He's not mad at you."

The boy cried harder. Words were coming through the sobs, but God alone knew what they were. God and Bobby, that is. "He wants you to find his daddy and bring him home," Bobby said.

"Me?"

"The other preacher used to do that sometimes."

The next morning Philip began calling—the police, the hospital, the Salvation Army shelter. No one knew anything about Richard Slaytor's whereabouts, although the Salvation Army had met up with him before and promised to keep an eye out. Well, it was the best he could do. There was still the Christmas Eve service to prepare for, and Grace needed him to help complete the preparations at home. The children and their families were coming over Christmas afternoon.

He was working frantically and tardily on his sermon for the evening and had given strict orders that he was not to be disturbed when the boys appeared. He never knew how they got past his secretary, but they did. Bobby had Wayne by the hand, and Wayne was dragging the one-armed bear.

"Didn't find him yet, huh, Reverend?"

"No"—Philip cleared his throat—"I called and called. No one has seen him." Bobby stepped forward. "We figured you need a picture."

"A picture?"

"Yeah. How you going to know it's him if you don't

have no picture?" The boy handed him a faded snapshot of a smiling young couple at the beach. "That's him." Bobby pointed to the man in the swimming trunks. "The other one's my mother."

"I see."

"I done wrote out all the information on the back." He turned the photo over. In smudged pencil Philip read:

Mr. Richard Slaytor
3476 Fifth St. Apt. 4-D Tel. 465—6879
Eyes blue Hair brown Size tall

"That's so you can identify him."

"I see."

"Wayne want to know if you need the bear back."

"No, no. That's all right, Wayne. I think I can manage without the bear, thank you."

He must be out of his mind. It was nearly dark. He had a midnight service that he wasn't ready for. His wife was having guests for supper. And here he was, walking the city streets, peering into doorways, showing a faded snapshot to drunks. "Do you know this man? Have you seen him lately?"

As he showed the picture, the stench would assault his nostrils. Several times he thought he would surely be sick and would have to turn hurriedly away. He tried bartenders and passersby, and as the evening wore on and he got more desperate, he approached the streetwalkers. First, they would flash him their sugar-hard smiles and then sneer when he made clear his mission.

It was so cold, his face hurt. He was tired of walking and

bending and begging. There was no kindness in the street. The faces he met were as hard and chilled as the concrete beneath his feet. A damp wind snaked up the sleeves of his overcoat and pierced him through.

"Merry Christmas, Pop!"

He had only time to puzzle over the youngster's greeting before the crashing blow hit his head and he crumpled to the pavement.

His first thought as he woke, the room spinning around him, was that he had died. So, this is what death is like, he was saying to himself matter-of-factly, when the pain surged and he had to blink hard against it. He was lying on a hard, very narrow cot. The smell was that of strong disinfectant, and the sight, when the pain allowed him to look at all, was that of bars. Then the pain surged, and he closed his eyes once more. When the pain ebbed slightly, he began to feel something else. He was dead, all right. He was dead and in Hell, but it was all right. Something—someone—some powerful presence was there with him. He was not afraid—not afraid, that is, of death or of Hell—but strangely afraid of the presence. He was both afraid and not afraid. He wanted to call out, "Who are you? What are you doing here?" But he was silent because he both knew and did not know the answer.

Then there was a voice. A perfectly ordinary human voice that said, "Your wife is here to take you home."

Poor Grace! What must she be thinking? He had called her once to tell her not to wait supper. Someone helped him to his feet, opened the door of the cage, and supported him down a hall lined with cages into a room so bright with light that he could hardly stand it.

He was dimly aware that there was a woman waiting, but he couldn't bear to open his eyes in that bright place.

"That ain't my husband," the woman's voice said. "My Lord! It's the reverend."

Philip sat down. He had to. He was afraid he might start giggling. He was so tired and his head hurt so much that he wasn't sure he could control himself.

She began to swear at the police. "The poor man got mugged. Look at that bump on his head. Lord, don't you guys ever look before you drag somebody to jail?" She bent over him solicitously. "Don't you know better than to wander round after dark in a neighborhood like this? You could get hurt, Reverend."

He was too tired to reply. The police produced the snapshot with the address on the back. "This was all he had on him. I guess they stole everything else."

"Where'd you get this picture?" she asked Philip.

"The boys—"

"Lord. Lord. You was out looking for Slaytor when they got you, right, Reverend? Did you ever hear the like?" she demanded. "Christmas Eve and the preacher is out looking for some no good man 'cause his baby wants him home for Christmas." She shook her head. "If that don't beat all. We better get you to the emergency room and let them look at that bump."

"No," he said. He was feeling a little more in control. "I've got a midnight service. Just call a taxi and get me back to the church. I'll check with a doctor tomorrow."

He was never able to explain about the service. It might have been the injury, which proved to be a mild concussion, but it couldn't have been only that. As he stood up and looked out over his beautiful, warmly dressed congregation, he saw among them a woman and two little boys and a one-armed bear. He had failed them, but there they were. They had understood. Even Wayne was smiling up at him, waiting to hear the Christmas story of God who not only accepts the sacrifice of a broken and contrite heart, but of God who is himself broken.

He descended into Hell. Philip didn't say so aloud, but suddenly he knew what the words meant. Born in a stinking barn, friend of the poor, the prostitute, the thief—broken at last on a cross. He descended into Hell. And just for a while, maybe for just this once in Philip's usually proper and comfortable life, God had let him be there, too. I know, Philip wanted to cry to those who sat before him, I know what it is. Right, Lord? Didn't you let me see a glimpse of your glory?

Just then Wayne held up the bear and made it wave its one remaining paw toward the pulpit. It was like a great Amen from a heavenly choir. God had not despised his puny little sacrifice. Philip's heart swelled with a joy that had no words except, "Glory, glory, glory, to God in the highest, and on earth peace, good will toward men."

My Name Is Joseph

In the sixth month the angel Gabriel was sent from God to a city of Galilee named Nazareth, to a virgin betrothed to a man whose name was Joseph, of the house of David; and the virgin's name was Mary.

My name is Joseph. In Spanish I am called José. But I have not always spoken Spanish. I learned it from the old priest who came to our mountain village when I was a boy. My people are Indians, descendants of the great Maya. Our civilization is older than the Christian era. The priest said I should be very proud, but it is hard to be proud when your belly is empty.

Before I was born our people owned rich farmlands, but a *yanqui* company needed those lands for coffee, and since we were only Indians, the government moved us deeper into the mountains to land no one else wanted.

My parents were dead, so the priest became a father to me. He taught me to read and write, and the year after his coming, at the Feast of the Annunciation, he baptized me. It was he who named me José. He told me that just as Joseph was given the care of the infant Jesus, so I must always care for those weaker than myself.

When I was a boy, I obeyed him and helped him, but as a young man I became rebellious. It was hard enough to get food for myself—how could I worry about others? I know it must have saddened the heart of my foster father to see me go down to the coffee plantations at harvest time to make a little money and then waste it on drink and women in the town. Seven years ago, I returned to the village after the harvest to find that the old priest had died.

At first I was pleased. I am ashamed to say it now, but with him gone there was no one to look sad and shake his head at my behavior. And besides, he had left his house to me. It was not large, but it was all mine. It only took a few days to discover the rest of my inheritance. He had left me the entire village. Everyone who was sick or hungry or afraid would come to my door.

"Go away!" I said to them. "I am not a priest. The priest is dead."

"You can read," an old woman said to me. "The father taught you. You must be our priest now. We have no other."

Little by little, whether it was my own guilt or the Spirit of God, I became the leader of my village. I did not perform the Mass, of course, but they pleaded with me until I read the sacred words to them each week. At night, after the day's work was done, those who wanted to learn would gather in my little house, and I would try to teach them to read from the old priest's Spanish Bible. Since most of them did not speak Spanish, only the Indian dialect of our village, this was a discouraging task. But they were grateful and gave me gifts of maize or beans that they would not allow me to refuse.

My wife, Elena Maria, was one of my pupils. She was a clever, bright-eyed young girl, who learned quickly and soon began to help me with the others. We were married and in five years had two sons and a third child on the way.

I have not mentioned the political situation in my country in those days. Our village was quite remote, you see. The soil was poor, and there was no true road. We were many days' walk from the nearest coffee plantations, and at least five miles from another Indian village. It had been a long time since anyone in our village had had enough surplus to make the long journey to market.

I, who used to go farther down the mountain to work, no longer left the village. There was too much to do. We had begun to work together. We shared seed and combined our tiny plots into larger fields to grow our beans and maize more efficiently and to let some of the land rest and recover its strength. A farmer I had met some years before in the town had told me this secret.

I was hoeing maize in the large village field the day I saw guerrillas coming up the side of the mountain. I did not know at first that they were guerrillas. I could see only a band of Indians—say twenty-five or so—climbing up toward us. As the leader of my village, I went down to meet them, followed by my people. Then I saw the old rifles slung over their shoulders and the machetes hung at their belts. There were both men and women; some were almost children; four or five were old enough to be fathers to me.

"Why do you come with guns?" I asked. I had to sound very brave because my people were standing just behind me.

"We do not come to harm you, my brother." The leader of the band was a man my own age. "We come to warn you. The soldiers are searching the mountain villages for communists."

"We have nothing to fear," I said. "There are no communists among us." I was, in fact, the only one in the village who knew what the word *communist* meant.

"Who is your leader?"

"You are speaking to him," I said.

"Are you a catechist?" the man asked.

"I teach my people what I know," I answered. "We have no priest."

"Your children look better fed than most."

"It is because we help each other in this village," I said, not without a little pride.

"You teach people to read and write, and you cooperate in your farming?"

"Yes," I said. His question seemed foolish to me.

"For this, my brother," he said softly, "they will call you a communist, and they will kill you. You had better join us."

But I did not go with them. I was Joseph, given the care of the weak and the young. I had no stomach for rifles and fighting. Besides, I did not know these people. They might well be lying.

A week later a single stranger made her way up the mountain. She was from a village fifty miles to the south and west of us. She asked which direction the guerrillas had gone. Elena, seeing how tired and hungry the visitor was, took her to our house and gave her food. The woman gave us her story. The soldiers had come to her village and demanded to know where the communists were being hidden.

"We knew no communists," the woman said. "We had heard rumors of a guerrilla band in the mountains behind us, but none of us had seen them. The soldiers refused to believe us. They took our five strongest men away in their truck. Next day, we found their mutilated bodies in the road." She stopped speaking for a moment. We waited in silence. "One of them," she said, "was my husband.

"The soldiers came again. 'See how cruel the communists are,' they said. 'We questioned your men and let them go. Now those villains have slaughtered them—'" She stopped again, fixing her eyes on my two-year-old son resting in his mother's lap. "I was crazy with grief, so I shouted, 'You lie! You did this crime yourselves!' They killed my children before my eyes with their machetes. Then they raped me and left me for dead." Her eyes flashed with hatred. "I go now to join the rebellion in the mountains. Tell me where they are!"

We could not tell her, but the following day she went on, leaving dread behind her like dense fog on the mountain.

We had one more warning. Another woman, from the village nearest to our own, told me that if I did not leave, the whole village would suffer. But how could I flee alone without my sons and Elena? We left together, taking almost nothing, because we knew the children would tire quickly and we would have to carry them.

And Joseph also went up from Galilee, from the city of Nazareth, to Judea, to the city of David, which is called Bethlehem, because he was of the house and lineage of David, to be enrolled with Mary, his betrothed, who was with child.

I thought of Joseph, my namesake, as we crossed the mountains, traveling north in the cold mists of darkness. We were afraid to travel by day. When light came, we would lie crouched under the cover of foliage, sometimes sleeping, sometimes listening to a helicopter searching the mountainsides for signs of those in hiding there. I have heard of the black slaves of your own country, who followed the North Star to freedom. In the Scriptures, it is the wise men that follow the star, but I did not feel very wise. I, Joseph, whose wife was great with child, was searching, not for the land of my forefathers but for some place, any place where my child might be born in safety.

We ran out of food within three days. We had tried to be careful, but the children were hungry, and we could not let them cry. Someone might hear.

God sent angels to watch over us. One was an old man hunting birds. We came upon his solitary fire one night, too hungry for proper caution.

"Ah, my children," he said, "my little children, God did not mean for you to suffer so." And he fed us roasted dove and beans wrapped in tortillas, and we shared his cup of boiled coffee. It was the first time I had seen the little boys smile since we left our village.

"There are some of our people in hiding two days' walk from here," he told us. "They will help you get into Mexico." Our angel gave us beans and tortillas and a little meat for our journey.

We walked for three nights, seeing no one, but at dawn on the third day, the lookout for the guerrilla camp found us and led us to his compatriots. I did not know these people. It was a different band from those who had come through our village. The leader was a young woman. She asked my name. When I told her, she said, "I have heard this name. They are searching for you." Her words chilled me because I knew that my people had suffered because of me. And that was true. Many had died. Our pigs and goats and foodstuffs had been stolen. The village was burned.

I should have stayed, I thought. I should have died for them. But how could I have stayed and caused my wife and sons to die as well? I am not God that I can weigh one life against another. Surely, as the hunter said, God did not mean for any of us to suffer so. What harm have we done that we should be punished? We only ask to be left alone to live out our humble lives as God wills, to bring our children into the world without fear.

We did not dream of riches or power—only that our little ones might lie down at night without the pain of an empty stomach.

"Why don't you join us?" the young woman said, seeing how I grieved for my village.

But I could not. Perhaps it was only selfishness, perhaps distaste for killing, but I wanted to take my sons and my wife and my child not yet acquainted with the sorrows of this world—I wanted to take them to a place of peace. Then if I died, it would not matter. They would know that I had been Joseph to them.

"I cannot help you now," I said to the leader, "but if you help me, perhaps someday God will let me repay you." She was not happy to hear my decision, but there were already many children to care for in their camp, so the guerrillas gave us food and directions to a convent just over the border.

"They will feed you there," she said, "and find you a place to live."

I thought once we crossed into Mexico we would be safe. I cannot tell you how light my heart was the night we came to the convent. It was the Feast Day of Saint Nicholas, and as we celebrated our first Mass in many years, I rejoiced. Saint Nicholas had loved the poor. Surely, he would aid us. After Mass, the sisters fed us a warm meal of red beans and rice. They gave us hot water to bathe with and clean cots to sleep upon. We felt we had reached heaven itself.

The next day we learned differently. We could not live in that village. Soldiers had come just two nights before. They had followed refugees across the border, dragged them from the houses where they had sought to hide, put them in trucks, and headed south. Their bodies had been left along the border as a warning both to those who might wish to flee and to those tempted to take them in. There were "ears" in the village, the sisters told me, informers who told our soldiers when strangers came to the village. And the Mexican police could not, or would not, protect fugitives.

"Elena and I speak Spanish," I said. "We will pretend to be Mexican Indians."

"Your children will betray you," the Reverend Mother said sadly. "They are too young. They will forget and speak their own dialect." I knew she was right.

The sisters gave us a huge basket of food, a little money, and tickets for buses going north. They took away our beautiful woven Indian garments and dressed us as poor Mexicans. Last of all they gave Elena a large bag of sweets. "You must keep the children's mouths full of candy," the Reverend Mother said, "so they will not speak."

And while they were there, the time came for her to be delivered. And she gave birth to her firstborn son and wrapped him in swaddling cloths, and laid him in a manger, because there was no place for them in the inn.

On that long trip from La Trinitaria to Nuevo Laredo, I thought often of the child that Elena carried. My first hope, of course, was that he would not choose to be born on a bus—that he would wait until we reached the safety of the

Benedictine community that had promised to care for us. In our village, birthing is women's work; I did not want Elena to have to count on me when her hour came. And if we had to stop, had to ask for help, how long could we keep our nationality secret?

But God is good. When Mexican police boarded the bus we rode, Elena and I pretended to sleep and prayed that the wide-eyed boys, their mouths bulging with sweets, would not speak. How many times did we change from one crowded, dirty bus to another? I cannot remember. I only remember the young man who came up to me when we got off the last bus in Nuevo Laredo. He spoke my name softly. When I nodded, he said, "Follow me."

At the community they greeted us with great kindness. "Poor little mother," they said of Elena. "We must get her across the Rio Grande as soon as possible. The children you can keep quiet, but an infant—"

How could I ask her to travel farther? I looked at my once beautiful young wife, her body sagging with the weight of the child and her own exhaustion. Did they know how many nights she had walked, how many days and nights she had ridden? "Let us stay until after the New Year," I begged. "In January, when the child is still tiny and will hardly make a sound . . ."

But it was Elena who persuaded me. "If the child is born in the United States," she argued, "he is a citizen. They cannot send a citizen to an alien land to die. A citizen has many rights. The sister told me."

And so it was arranged. An American priest was coming with a young man, his nephew. They would be driving a van. In the back of the van, the young man had built a bed. They would take out the side of the bed, and we would climb under it and be nailed in. Tiny holes had been drilled close to the mattress so that we would have air to breathe. I was terrified by such a plan. Suppose, despite the candy, one of the boys would cry out in fright? Suppose Elena's time came? Suppose the border guards discovered us and sent us back to our homeland?

I saw the young man and his uncle the priest just minutes before I helped my family into our hiding place and crawled in behind them. The youth was chewing gum and wearing cowboy boots. A most unlikely angel, I thought. But the Reverend Mother introduced him to me. "This is Christopher," she said. I remembered the joy I had felt on Saint Nicholas's Day. God was sending me still another sign—Christopher, the Christ bearer, the saint who carried the infant Jesus to safety when Herod pursued the Holy Family. He would deliver us from harm.

It may seem like blasphemy to you, but as I lay there in the darkness, aware of each shallow breath from the bodies of my dear ones pressed so closely against my own, feeling the movement of the child in Elena's womb, my heart went out to this one yet unborn. It was not the firstborn—it was not even perhaps a son—and I was not a righteous man, but somehow that innocent life was Jesus to me. I, Joseph, hiding in the dark, was powerless, but surely God must protect his own.

I could hear the muffled voices of our benefactors. I knew when they stopped and paid the bridge toll. I could tell from the growl of many engines and the choking smell of petrol that the bridge was crowded with holiday traffic. We must not cough, no matter how noxious the fumes. The van moved forward so slowly, so terribly slowly. Elena shifted against me. I realized that she was stroking the boys, hoping they would sleep.

At last we came to the border. I heard a strange North American voice—the police. He was asking questions at the window. The priest and Christopher got out. My heart stopped beating. "Holy God, holy God," I said to myself over and over, the only prayer I could manage. Someone opened the back doors of the van. I waited for the jolt that would tell me the policeman had boarded and would begin his search. I did not dare even to reach my hand to my wife or to try to cover my younger son's mouth. I lay there frozen, waiting.

The doors banged shut. The van shuddered. No one had climbed aboard. The front doors opened and then closed. I heard English words even I could understand. "Okay, Father. Merry Christmas to you." The van moved forward, slowly at first, and then gradually up to a normal speed. Beside me I could feel Elena's body heave with sobs she still did not dare let loose. I, too, was crying.

Our daughter was born later that same night, not in a stable—in the back of a 1978 Plymouth van, thirty miles south of San Antonio, Texas. In the end it was I who held out my hands and welcomed her tiny wet body into this world and cut the cord with the Father's pocket knife. Neither the priest, nor the one called Christopher, dared to perform this simple office. I laughed; how easy, how joyful it was to greet this infant. I was singing with the angels, "Gloria, gloria, gloria."

I wrapped her in a blanket the nuns had given me and held her for her brothers and her rescuers to see. "Her name is Esperanza," I said.

"*Esparanza* means hope," the priest explained to young Christopher.

"Hope." I tried this new English word in my mouth. It

tasted sweeter than the children's candy. I looked up at the bright stars—the same ones shining down on the mountains of my ruined village. "Someday," I said to the infant in my arms, "someday peace will come to our mountains, and I will take you there. Hope will come to my people."

Until then, with the help of God and His saints, and all the holy angels, I will watch over this blessed child.

My name is Joseph.

Woodrow Kennington Works Practically a Miracle

"The first thing I see when I open the door is Sara Jane lying on the rug with my stamp collection all over the place." Woodrow was sitting on the curb in front of his house trying to explain the tragic events of the past hour to his friend Ralph. "My stamp collection!"

Ralph was doing his best to sound sympathetic. "Geez," he said.

"I start screaming like an idiot, 'What the hell you think you're doing?' She says—you know how she sticks up her eyebrow—only five-year-old I ever heard of could poke up one eyebrow—she says, cool as can be, 'Hi, Whoodrow.' Blowing my name out like birthday candles. 'Hi, Whoodrow. I'm playing post office.' *Post office!*" Woodrow bent over in pain. "Post office with practically priceless stamps I inherited from my grandfather. I was practically crying out loud. 'Why? Why?'" Woodrow spread out both arms, imitating himself. "'Why are you playing post office with my stamps?'"

"And she says?"

"She says—get this—she says, 'Don't be stoopid, Whoodrow. You gotta have stamps to play post office.'"

"Oh, yeah?" Ralph grinned and poked him in the ribs with an elbow. "Just ask Jennifer Leonard."

"Shut up, Ralph. You haven't even heard the worst part yet."

Ralph tried to get properly serious. "There's a worst part?"

"About this time my mother comes rushing in, in a bathrobe. It is three thirty in the afternoon. My sister has destroyed an entire fortune in rare stamps while my mother has been taking a nap."

"Yeah?"

"The *reason* she has been taking a nap and let my juvenile-delinquent sister run wild—she takes me off to the den and shuts the door to tell me this goody—the reason she laid down and took her eye off Sara Jane 'for one minute' is that she is pregnant."

"Yeah?"

"My mother is thirty-eight years old."

"So?"

"Ralph, she is too old already to handle Sara Jane."

At about eight that evening Ralph called. After the usual questions about homework had been taken care of, he said, "You know I been thinking about what you told me. I don't think you should be too upset."

"Ralph! That was a practically priceless stamp collection!"

"No, I don't mean about the stamps. I mean about

becoming a brother again. Wood, face it. You got no place to go but up, man. When this next kid is five, you're seventeen. Seventeen. You know what a seventeen-year-old guy looks like to a five-year-old? Geez. This kid is liable to worship you."

It was not the worst idea Ralph had ever had. In fact, the more Woodrow thought about it, the better it sounded. His mother was surprised and delighted when he started going out of his way to help her. She began to treat him more and more like an adult. She even asked him to try to get Sara Jane to accept the idea of a new baby.

This was no small problem. Sara Jane had expressed neither excitement nor resentment when they told her. She simply pretended that she hadn't heard. Once when he was babysitting, Woodrow tried very hard to explain the whole situation to her. He even threw in a few interesting facts of life as a bonus.

"Don't be stoopid, Whoodrow." She never mentioned the subject again, or even seemed to hear others mention it, until the day she found Woodrow and his mother putting together the old baby bed in her room.

She marched in, hands on hips. "Get this junk outta my room."

"Sara Jane, it's for the baby." Mother was super patient. "You remember, I talked to you yesterday . . . "

"I'm not having no baby."

"We're all having a baby, Sara Jane."

"Not me."

"OK. *I'm* having a baby, but . . ."

"Then put this junk in your own room."

"But darling, I explained, there's no place. . . ."

Woodrow offered on the spot to take the baby into his room. His mother stalled and his father fumed, but eventually the bed, bureau, and rocking chair took the place of his racing-car setup. His father bought a screen and covered it with airline posters, but he needn't have. Woodrow was not feeling anything like a martyr. It was the chance of a lifetime. He would start this kid out right. No more Sara Janes for him.

As for Sara Jane, she would come to Woodrow's door and stand there with her hands on her hips, her eyebrow elevated, staring at the crib legs peeking out below the bottom of the screen, but she never said a word. Occasionally, though, she would sigh—a sigh as long and weary as the *whooo-oosh* of his mother's ancient percolator. It made Woodrow uneasy, but not prepared for what happened next. He wondered later if he should have been prepared. Shouldn't he have taken a cue from her strange shift in TV programs? What normal kid would move in the span of two weeks from *Electric Company* to *Speed Racer* to, of all things, *The One True Word*, starring Brother Austin Barnes? He had really meant to ask her about it, but the switch took place in the last wild days before the baby was born, and frankly, everyone was so glad to have her quiet and occupied that they neglected to keep a proper check on what she was watching.

When his father called from the hospital at seven o'clock to tell him that he had a brother, Woodrow let out a whoop that could have been heard for blocks. It brought Sara Jane out of the den into the kitchen. "It's a boy!" Woodrow yelled at her. "A boy!"

She watched him with a very peculiar expression on her face—neither anger nor surprise, certainly not delight. Where had he seen it before? A memory of old fading pictures in the back of the Sunday school closet came to his mind—it was that same sickly sweet half smile.

Then she let him have it. "Brother Whoodrow," she said. "I saw Jesus today."

"You what?"

Her smile, if anything, got more sickly. "I said, 'I saw Jesus.'"

Surely it was that religious program she had been watching—that combined with the shock of the news he had just given her. He felt very generous, almost sorry for her, so he tried to be kindly. "So you saw Jesus, huh?"

"I was walking home from school. All alone. Nobody meets me halfway anymore. Mommy got too fat, and Mrs. Judson is too lazy." She paused to let these sad words sink in. "But Jesus loves me. Just like Brother Austin says. When Jesus saw me coming home from school, he stopped his big black car. 'Hi,' he says."

"Sara Jane, that wasn't Jesus. He never had any big black car."

"He does now."

Woodrow was beginning to feel panicky. "Did he ask you to get into the car or anything?"

"No," she said primly.

He was not about to let Sara Jane get kidnapped while his mother was in the hospital. He told Mrs. Judson, who was staying there days, that Sara Jane had to be met at the school door. Mrs. Judson read one of those newspapers that never hesitate to give all the gory details, so when he told her about the big black car, she made the trip to the kindergarten door every day, lazy or not.

In the meantime, Daniel came home. He was the greatest baby in the world, even when he cried. In fact, Woodrow's favorite time was when Daniel cried at two o'clock in the morning. His mother would fuss and apologize when she'd come in and find Woodrow awake, but then they'd talk while she fed the baby. What a warm, good feeling to be talking in the middle of the night—grown-up to grown-up. It would have been the happiest time of his life except for Sara Jane.

He may have saved her from kidnapping, but he certainly hadn't solved the real problem. He wasn't sure if he was going to be able to stand it. Sara Jane the screaming baby, he had endured. Sara Jane the unbearable brat, he had gotten more or less used to. But Sara Jane the Saint was about to do him in.

Ralph thought it was the funniest thing since Whoopee cushions, but he didn't have to live with her. She was always smiling at him and calling him Brother Whoodrow and begging him to watch *The One True Word* with her. She prayed all the time. If Mrs. Judson fussed at her, she would go into her room and fall on her knees, praying that God would forgive poor bad Mrs. Judson. It was Woodrow's job to fix breakfast for the two of them. Sara Jane would bless the food until the toast had turned to floor tile.

But even that he might have put up with had she not announced to him one morning that their parents were going to Hell.

"Shut up, Sara Jane."

"But they're lost!" she said.

"They are not lost. They're Presbyterians."

"See? They don't even know they're lost and going to Hell."

"Well, why don't you just tell them?"

"They'd laugh at me."

They would, too. He wanted to laugh himself, but he

couldn't quite. Suppose his father and mother were headed for Hell and didn't even know it? Suppose he were? They were all bound for Hell while Sara Jane . . . Suddenly, as the robots would say, it did not compute. Sara Jane the Saint was pure plastic—the fake of all fakes. Instead of letting her scare him, he should be whipping her back into shape. It was up to him to get her back to normal. Normal, mind you, was never all that great, but normal he could manage.

First, he would silence *The One True Word*. Fortunately, the TV set was practically an antique, which meant all he had to do was unplug the little gizmo that the government made you get a couple of years ago to make your old set work at all. Just to be safe, he took it and hid it in his underwear drawer.

When Sara Jane complained to her father that the TV was broken, he hardly looked up from his newspaper. He didn't like TV anyhow, which was why he'd never bothered to get a decent set.

"Who is going to fix the TV?" she persisted.

Her father put down his paper. "Nobody has time to bother with that TV before Christmas. Besides"—he was already back behind the paper—"you watch too much TV anyway."

Woodrow found her some minutes later on her knees in the den, her hand on the cold set. "O Lord"— Woodrow wasn't sure if she were praying aloud for his benefit or God's—"O Lord, make this TV set well. The Devil broke it, but you can make it well."

"Sara Jane!" He was so shocked that he burst right into her prayer. She ignored him and kept on rocking and praying. Woodrow was not crazy about being called the Devil, but he sure as heck was not going to plug it back up and turn the kid into a permanent religious weirdo.

The next morning at breakfast, there were no lengthy announcements. Sara Jane just rolled her eyes up at the ceiling and said, "OK, God. You know what you gotta do." And in answer to Woodrow's openmouthed stare, she said, "He knows if he doesn't hurry up and fix that set, I'm not going to believe in him anymore."

When he came in from school two days in a row to find her praying over the TV set, he began to weaken. "How about me taking you Christmas shopping, Sara Jane?"

Slowly she turned and gave him her saddest face. "I guess I'm not going to believe in Christmas this year. The TV still doesn't work."

"Oh"—his voice sounded very cheery and very fakey—"I wouldn't give up on Christmas just because of some old TV. Maybe it's just a lose connection or something."

"God can do anything he wants to. If he doesn't want to fix this TV, it means he doesn't want me to be his child. I guess nobody wants me to be their child."

Ralph, after he stopped laughing, suggested that Woodrow launch a campaign. It was obvious that the child felt insecure. Woodrow needed to prove to her that her family really loved her. Then she would be cured.

Woodrow was desperate enough to try anything, even a suggestion from Ralph. He persuaded his mother that she was not too tired to make cookies with Sara Jane, since he, Woodrow, would clean up the entire kitchen afterward. Sara Jane made twelve gorgeous gingerbread men, all scowling.

Woodrow talked his father into taking Sara Jane on a special trip to see Santa Claus. She had climbed, after much urging, onto the old fellow's lap, only to ask him why his breath smelled all mediciney. Woodrow himself devoted a full Saturday morning to helping Sara Jane make a crèche out of baker's dough.

"Sara Jane." He tried not to sound too critical. "We can't use fourteen snakes in one manger scene."

"That's all I feel like making, Whoodrow. Just snakes and snakes"—she sighed—"dead snakes."

"Suppose," he said, his eyes carefully on the sheep he was modeling, "suppose the TV would get well. Would you feel better then?"

"It's too late. God flunked already."

"Maybe he just needed a little more time, or something."

She looked him dead in the eye. "If the TV got fixed now, I'd know it was you or daddy did it. Just to shut me up. You're just scared I'm going to mess up your old Christmas. That's all you care about."

He tried to protest, but she was too close to the truth. How could he enjoy Christmas when he felt like some kind of a monster?

Christmas Eve their parents went off to church, leaving him in charge. There had been a bit of trouble earlier when Sara Jane had refused at first to hang up her stocking. "I just don't believe in Christmas anymore," she had said wearily. Their parents hadn't known whether to take her seriously or not, but Woodrow had. He whispered in her ear that if she didn't hang up her stocking that minute he was going to beat the

you-know-what out of her the minute the folks walked out
the door. She sighed, that long now-frequent sigh of hers,
and handed him her stocking to put up.

After he had gotten her, still moaning and sighing, into
bed, he sank into the big living-room chair, staring miserably
at the blinking lights of the Christmas tree. The tree itself
looked so fat and jolly and merry that he was close to tears
when the telephone rang.

It was Ralph. He was baby-sitting, too, but he was so
cheerful it made Woodrow feel murderous. "Say, there's this
great movie on Channel Seven. It was practically X-rated
when it first came out."

"Our TV's broken, remember?"

Ralph chortled. "I also remember, old buddy, that you
can work that little miracle whenever you want to."

Woodrow slammed down the receiver. Everything
always seemed simple to Ralph. When Ralph looked at his
Christmas tree, he didn't have to see at its base fourteen
dead snakes guarding a manger scene. If only he could fix
everything as easily as he could fix that blasted TV. Well,
what the heck? A practically X-rated movie was sure to take
his mind off Sara Jane for a little while.

He moved the TV around so he could put the plugs for
the little box back into it. The old set warmed as slowly as
ever, gradually filling the den with the sound of Christmas
music. He reached out to switch the channel, but before he
could do so, the hundred-voiced TV choir sang a line that
made his fingers stop in midair.

"See him in a manger laid whom the angels praise
above. . . ."

I saw Jesus today. That's what Sara Jane had said that had
started this whole mess. What was so wrong, after all, with

a lonesome little kid, even a bad—maybe especially a bad—little lonesome kid wanting some proof that God cared about her? It was not as if she were twelve and needed to face the facts. Maybe Ralph had an idea, after all. Maybe Woodrow could work a little miracle.

He took the hedge clipper out to the backyard and cut so much dried grass and weeds that it took him four or five trips to carry it all in. He dumped his underwear on the bed, put his pillow into the drawer, and covered it with grass. The rest of the grass and weeds he scattered across the living-room floor. He put the drawer on a footstool in front of the Christmas tree. The knobs were showing, so he turned it around. He turned off the blinking lights. The lighting had to be just so, or it wouldn't work. He tried a single candle on the end table. Better. He experimented with the music from the TV in the den until he got it just loud enough to sound sort of mysterious. Then, very carefully, his heart thumping madly against his chest, he lifted the still-sleeping Daniel from his bed, wrapped him in a crib sheet, and laid him in the drawer. When he was satisfied that everything was perfect, he wrapped his own top sheet around himself and went to get Sara Jane.

He shook her and then stepped back near the door. "Sara Jane!" He made his voice strong and slightly spooky. "Sara Jane!" She stirred in her sleep. "Sara Jane Kennington!"

Slowly Sara Jane sat up.

"Sara Jane!" She was looking around trying to figure out, perhaps, where the voice was coming from, so he hiked up his sheet and spread his arms out wide. "Arise!" he commanded. "Arise and follow me!"

Now she saw him—at least she turned and looked straight at him—but when she slid out of bed and padded toward the door, it was as though she were sleepwalking. He turned quickly and led her down the hall. Just as they got to the doorway into the living room, he stepped back and gestured for her to go ahead.

She went on for a few steps and then stopped. He watched her back. Her thin little body was shivering under her pajamas. Her head moved back and forth very slowly. She was taking the whole scene in. And it was beautiful. Even when you knew. Like that painting of the shepherds in the dark barn where the only light comes from the manger. The baby had worked his arms and legs loose from the sheet and was waving them in the air. Above the angel music you could hear his happy bubbling noises.

"Ohh." Sara Jane let out such a long sigh that her whole body shuddered. "Ohhh." She dared a tiny step forward. "Hi, Jesus," she said.

There was something so quiet, so pure, about the way she said it that it went straight through to Woodrow's stomach. He found he was shaking all over. Why was he so cold and scared? He had fooled her, hadn't he? He ought to be feeling proud, not sick to his stomach.

Sara Jane took another step toward the baby. Now what was he supposed to do? He hadn't given any thought to what he should do *after* the miracle. Stupid. Stupid. Stupid. He reached out to stop her from going any farther and stumbled over his sheet. "Oh, hell!"

She turned around, half afraid, half puzzled. "Whoodrow?"

"Don't be scared, Sara Jane. It's just me." He disentangled himself from the sheet. "Stoopid old Whoodrow." The choir from the den launched into a series of hallelujahs. "Oh, shut up!"

Sara Jane in the candlelight might have been a little princess waking from an enchanted sleep. Finally, she cocked her head. "Is that the TV?" she asked.

"Yeah." He turned on the 150-watt reading lamp. "I fixed it."

She blinked a moment in the brightness, and then marched over to the fake manger. "That's Daniel in there."

"Yeah." He was beginning to feel hot. "I was trying to fool you." He flopped heavily to the couch. "Sara Jane, for your future information, nobody should go around trying to fake miracles. First, I broke the TV so you wouldn't be religious, and then I fixed all this junk"—he waved his arm around the room—"so you would. Go ahead. Say it. I'm stoopid."

She came over to the couch and ducked her head so she could look up into his face. "This wasn't stoopid," she said. "I liked it."

She must not understand what he was trying to say. He repeated himself. "I was the one that broke the TV set in the first place."

"Huh?"

"I couldn't stand you praying and acting good all the time."

She looked surprised. "I thought you wanted me to be good, Whoodrow. You used to hate me when I was bad."

"I never hated you. Honest."

"Well"—she sighed her old weary sigh—"Mommy and Daddy did. They wouldn't have got a new one if they liked the old one."

His shame began to shift in the direction of the old exasperation. "Sara Jane Kennington, do you think they stopped liking me when you were born? Maybe they loved me even better than before."

"Really?" He thought she was going to smile, but instead her face clouded up. "Well, I know for sure God hates me. I been so bad." Her chin began to quiver. "I know for sure God hates me."

"Sara Jane. God is crazy about you."

First her eyebrow went up; then she giggled. "You're stoopid, Whoodrow."

"Maybe so," he said. "And then again, maybe not."

When he thought about it later, Woodrow wondered if his miracle had been so fake after all. Ralph's definition of a miracle was something that no one in his right mind would believe. And Ralph, for one, could not believe that Woodrow Kennington had spent Christmas Eve raking grass off his living-room floor while listening happily to his sister sing through practically the entire "Hallelujah Chorus" accompanied by a silver-voiced choir of thousands. In fact, now that Sara Jane was back to normal, he had some trouble believing it himself.

No Room in the Inn

In the winter, our house looks like a Christmas card. It's an old Vermont farmhouse nestled into the woods, with a view of the snow-covered Green Mountains. The attached barn is now a garage, and my parents run a bed-and-breakfast in the house. My dad works full-time at a computer outfit, so, being both the only man and the only kid at home, I spend a lot of time splitting wood, making fires in the huge kitchen woodstove, cleaning rooms, changing sheets, washing dishes—you name it.

When I saw my parents off at Burlington Airport last week, I tried to look a little sad—as a Christmas present to my mother, who was feeling terrible about leaving me alone for the holidays. Can you imagine? A sixteen-year-old boy alone in a country inn with no guests to cater to, no wood to split, no beds to make—nothing to do for ten glorious days but eat, sleep, and ski. And a new Lexus IS sitting in the other half of the garage whispering, "Use me! Use me! Use me!"

I had taken my folks to the airport in the 4 x 4. A good thing, too, because by the time I headed home, the snow was coming down hard. Great for the slopes, I thought, and switched on the radio, which was playing a sappy old-time number, "Let it Snow, Let it Snow, Let it Snow." I was feeling so good I listened to "White Christmas" and a jazzed-up version of "Away in a Manger" before I reached over to switch to my usual station. Ha! Ten days with no one complaining because I had switched the dial on the car radio.

I tried to figure out why I was feeling so great. Sure, I'd miss not having Christmas with the family. My sister's kids are terrific and they think their uncle Ben is God's gift to the world. But you have to understand. I never get time to myself these days. If I'm not working at school, I'm slaving away at the inn. It's really only a bed-and-breakfast, but my mother likes to call it the Inn. I'd have it all to myself, including the 4 x 4, which I have to share with my dad, and ta-da my mother's Lexus which for ten days was mine, all mine.

The euphoria had left me by the time I'd spent an hour and forty-five minutes driving what should have taken just over an hour. I was tired and hungry and feeling—could you believe it?—just a little bit sorry for myself in the blackness of a late winter afternoon when I turned off the interstate and headed for the village. I decided to stop at Gracie's, the only restaurant around, for meat loaf and cheer. Gracie is famous for both.

The woodstove was crackling warm, and the smell of meat loaf and homemade bread filled the place. There were a couple of farmers, Ewell Biggs and Ames Whitehead, sitting at the counter drinking coffee when I got there. They nodded at me as I sat down. I nodded back, waiting for Gracie's usual "Hello, stranger!" But Gracie just stared at me sadly. "It's meat loaf tonight," she said, as though that would be the last thing anyone would want.

"That's fine," I said, and then, "is something the matter, Gracie?"

"Gracie's all worried about them Russians," Ewell explained to me between slurps of coffee.

"They're Armenians," Gracie said to him, and then to me, "I was just watching the news. Five hundred thousand with no place to sleep, and it's cold."

"It ain't like Vermont winter," Ames said. "Lord, it was seventeen below at my barn this morning."

"It's cold enough," Gracie insisted. "I saw this old woman on TV last night. They showed her hands. She was kinda holding them tight like this"—Gracie clutched her hands together in front of her ample bosom—"and she didn't have any gloves. She was just holding onto herself and shivering. It killed me. I couldn't sleep last night thinking about that poor old woman."

I thought Gracie was going to burst into tears, but she pulled herself together enough to get me a huge steaming plate of meat loaf, mashed potatoes, and beans, with three hot rolls on the side. She knows how I love her rolls.

Just then I felt a blast of air on my back. We all turned to look at the door. A man was standing there—a stranger. There was several days' growth of stubble on his face. He had on worn jeans and a flimsy baseball jacket and no hat or gloves. He was not anyone from around here.

"Take a seat," Gracie said. "Be right with you." Before

I could ask for the ketchup, she was back to the Armenians. "And those children. Did you see those poor kids in the hospital with their legs all crushed? One little boy couldn't even remember who he was. The doctor didn't know if his parents were dead or alive."

I opened my mouth during the pause to ask for the ketchup, but by then she had turned to the stranger. "Now, what can I do for you?" she asked.

He was still standing in front of the door as though he couldn't remember what he'd come in for. "Coffee," he muttered at last. "To go."

"People who got through the earthquake are just freezing to death from the cold," Gracie went on as she filled a large Styrofoam cup from the coffee urn.

The man looked puzzled. "Armenians," I said. "She's all upset about the Armenians."

It was obvious he didn't know what we were talking about. "There was a big earthquake over there. They think about fifty to sixty thousand people died."

"And the rest are likely to." Gracie gave a huge sigh. "Right at Christmas. I can't get over those poor children. Cream and sugar?"

"Yeah," the man said. "Both. Double."

Gracie put two teaspoons of sugar and a huge dollop of cream into the cup and pushed on a lid. "That'll be sixty-three cents," she said as the man handed her a dollar bill. "This mason jar here is for the Armenians," she said, pointing to it. "I'm taking donations—if you'd like to put in your change . . ."

The man took the change she held out and stuffed it into the pocket of his jeans. "How far to Burlington from here?" he asked.

"Well," said Gracie—you could tell she was a little bit annoyed that the man didn't care anything about her Armenians—"you get back on the interstate, it's about forty miles."

"I just came from there," I said, sticking my two cents in like a fool. "Road's terrible."

"Ah, they'll plow soon," said Ewell.

"I need gas," the man said.

"Well, that might be more of a problem. Nothing open this time of night," Ames said.

The man shrugged. He looked at Gracie, but she ignored him, carefully refilling my water glass. "Ben," she said. "You feeling lonely in that big place, come have Christmas dinner here with me."

"Thanks, Gracie," I said, keeping my back to the stranger. "I just might."

I felt the cold air as he opened the door to go. He muttered something as he went out. It sounded like "Damned Armenians," but maybe I just imagined that. "Friendly soul," Ewell remarked.

"Not too worried about your Russians, either," Ames teased.

"Armenians," Gracie said looking sadder than ever, so when I was ready to go I stuffed all my change into the jar, even though I'd given her a twenty.

The first thing I did when I got back home was to hang out the No Vacancy sign. I wasn't likely to get any visitors on a night like this, but I wasn't taking any chances. I had the evening all planned: first a roaring fire in the woodstove, then a large bottle of Coke and a two-pound bag of potato chips, then three rented videos in a row, none of which I would have been able to watch had there been anyone else in the house.

I had no sooner popped the first DVD into the machine and settled back to watch when the doorbell rang . . . and rang . . . and rang. There was nothing to do but go answer. I put on the chain and opened the door a crack. "Sorry, no vacancy," I said, and then I saw it was the stranger from Gracie's.

"How about if I just stay in the garage?" he asked. "Like you said, the interstate is terrible, and it's freezing out here in the car."

It wasn't my problem. "Sorry," I said. "No vacancies. There's Woodley's just off the interstate."

"I already tried there," he said. "I ain't got sixty-five dollars."

"Well, if I could let you stay, which I can't, it's sixty-five here, too."

"Look, I'm just asking to stay in your garage, so I won't freeze to death. You'd let a stray dog into the garage, wouldn't you, on a night like this?"

I hesitated. I didn't really like his looks. Besides, the Lexus was in there. If anything happened to that car, my mother would kill me.

He smiled then—the kind of shifty-eyed smile that immediately makes you distrust someone. "Just think of me as one of them Armenians," he said.

He was right. Fake smile or not, he *would* freeze to death in his car on a night like this. "Okay," I said. "Wait. I'll have to get my car out to make room for yours." I closed the front door and carefully locked it before going out through the kitchen to the attached garage. I got in the 4 x 4, pushed the button for the electric door, and slowly backed out. A ten-year-old Chevrolet with rusted sides drove into the slot beside the Lexus. I got the old blankets out of the cargo area, then locked the 4 x 4 and hurried into the garage.

I put the blankets on the back of the Chevy. "Here's some blankets in case," I yelled as I pushed the button to close the door. I couldn't look at his old car. I couldn't think of the man out here when I had a roaring fire going in the kitchen. But I sure wasn't going to let him inside. People get robbed and beaten up for that kind of stupidity—murdered, even.

He didn't say anything, not even thanks. But it didn't matter. I gave him what he asked for—more than he asked for.

I went in and turned up the TV very loud. . . . I don't know how long the knocking had been going on before I finally heard it. "Yeah?" I yelled through the closed kitchen door.

"Daddy said, could I use the bathroom?"

I was so startled to hear a kid's voice, I opened the door. Sure enough, there stood a dirty, skinny, red-faced kid. "Daddy said you'd let me use the bathroom."

I just opened the door wider and let him in. What was I supposed to do? Tell the kid to go out in the snow? Sheesh. I shut the door behind him and led him to the downstairs powder room. "Don't use the towels," I warned.

I waited outside the bathroom for what seemed like ten minutes. What in the world was the kid up to? Finally, he came out, walking tall and straight backed like some little prince. He didn't say a word, not even thank you.

"You're welcome," I said loudly as I let him out the door, but he didn't look my way.

I just sat down. The guy hadn't said anything about any kid. I was sure he hadn't. I probably should call the welfare people or the police or somebody. I hadn't figured out what to do when there was another, softer knock on the kitchen door.

This time I just opened it. "You've been to the bathroom already," I started to say when I saw it was a different kid—a stringy-haired little girl with a nose rubbed raw. "Where did you come from?" I asked.

She whispered something.

"What?"

Again, I caught the word *bathroom*, so I shut the door and pointed her to the powder room. I didn't even bother to warn her about my mother's fancy guest towels. Somehow, I knew this was going to be a long night.

Before the kid had left the bathroom, there was another knock. I snatched open the door, all ready to give the guy a piece of my mind. But this time a woman stood there, holding a baby in a filthy rag of a blanket.

I couldn't believe it. This was like one of those circus acts where people just keep coming out of a car. "Would you warm it?" she asked. I looked down. She was handing me a baby bottle. It was about half full of frozen milk.

"You better do it," I said. I got her a saucepan, filled it with water, and turned on the burner. "The kid—the little girl's in the bathroom," I said, nodding in that direction. I waited, as patiently as I could, for the woman to test the milk on her wrist and shove the bottle into the baby's mouth, and for the little girl to finish wiping her grubby little hands on all four of Mom's embroidered Irish linen guest towels.

"Now," I said. "I'm very sorry, but you're going to have to go."

"It's cold out there," the little girl whined as I tried to gently urge her out the door.

"I know," I said grimly, going out with her around the Lexus toward the Chevy. The man was sitting there behind the wheel, with all the windows rolled up. I went to the driver's side and tapped, but he didn't roll the window down. He looked straight ahead. I banged louder. "You're going to have to go," I said. "This isn't going to work. You didn't tell me you had kids with you."

The man turned slowly and opened the window a crack. He gave me a look—it was the most sarcastic expression I've ever seen on a man's face. "Just pretend we're some of them Armenians," he said and rolled the window up again.

I stood there for a minute, trying to figure out what to do next. It was so quiet I could hear the soft sounds of the baby drinking its milk. The little girl was watching me from the other side of the Chevy with big scared eyes. The woman hadn't moved. She was still standing in the doorway, the baby cradled in her arms, a dark silhouette against the light streaming from the bright kitchen. ". . . 'Round yon Virgin Mother and Child . . ." A shiver went through me.

"I'm sorry," I said to her, and I really was. It wasn't her fault. "I'm sorry, but you're going to have to find someplace else. I don't own this place. I'm just taking care of it, and the owners wouldn't approve of me letting people stay in the garage."

No one moved, but the little girl began to whimper again.

"I think there's a shelter or something in Barre. I could call on the phone . . ."

Still no one moved.

I went back to the kitchen door and pressed the opener button on the wall. The garage light flashed on and the door rattled up. The woman jumped, and the little girl started crying in earnest. "I'm sorry," I said again, although I was beginning to feel more angry than sorry. That jerk had really taken advantage.

Just pretend we're some of them Armenians. The nerve. I watched the woman help the crying child into the backseat of the car and climb in after her. The baby's blanket caught on something and she jerked it free. I could hear a tearing sound. At the front window the boy sat, his nose flattened against the pane.

I waited but nothing happened. The man was just going to sit there. Anger washed away what guilt I might have felt. I went around to the man's window again. "If you don't move out of here," I said, "I'm calling the police."

The man acted as if he hadn't heard. Suppose he just stayed there and they all froze to death right in our garage? Imagine the headlines—NO ROOM IN THE INN: HOMELESS FAMILY FREEZES AT LOCAL B & B. "I'm not kidding," I shouted. "I'm calling the cops!"

Through the closed windows of the Chevy, I could hear the little girl crying.

"Come on!" I yelled to block out the sound. "Get outta here!"

Finally, he started the motor and began to back out slowly. I ran to the 4 x 4. As soon as the Chevy was out of the way, I was going to drive it in and close the door. The snow had stopped. The plows would be out soon. They'd be okay. An unheated barn was no place for a baby.

And then I heard myself. "Away in a manger, no crib for his bed." No room in the inn, not for two thousand lousy years. Never.

The Chevy had stalled in the driveway. I jumped out and ran to the driver's window and pounded on it again. He stopped grinding the starter and turned to give me his sarcastic look. "We're going," he said.

"I changed my mind."

Now he opened the window. "What you say?"

"Put your car back in and come on in the house. It's freezing out here." He smiled grimly. "Thinking about them Armenians, huh?"

"No," I said. "Actually, I was thinking about something else."

I led the way into the kitchen and found them chairs so they could sit around the stove and get warm. Then I went to the phone to call Gracie. I knew I needed help, and she was sure to come. I'd just tell her I had a houseful of Armenians.

The Handmaid of the Lord

People think when your father is the minister that you get special favors, like you were God's pet or something. Rachel, for one, knew absolutely, positively that it was not true. God didn't love her better than Jason McMillan, who was getting an entire set of Mighty Morphin Power Rangers for Christmas. God didn't love her better than that Carrie Wilson, who was getting a new Barbie dollhouse with two new dolls, outfits included. Not that Rachel really wanted a Barbie dollhouse, or Power Rangers either, for that matter, but it was the principle of the thing. Carrie and Jason were getting what they asked Santa Claus for. When Rachel asked Santa for a horse, John and Beth just rolled their eyes. John and Beth were her older brother and sister. Beth was eleven and John, thirteen, and they thought they knew everything.

"But where would we keep a horse, Rachel?" her mother had asked. She was changing baby David's diapers and not paying Rachel much attention. "We live in the church manse. You know how small our yard is."

"Rachel," her father had said in his most patient voice, "what is Christmas really about? If all you think about is Santa Claus, you're going to miss the main event." Rachel's heart sank. When your father told you to think what Christmas was *really* about, she knew what that meant. It meant no horse. Not even a pony. Ministers' kids never got really good presents at Christmas. She should know that by now. It didn't count if you were naughty or nice. Gregory Austin had pulled the alarm last Sunday and made the fire trucks come in the middle of church service, but he was getting his own personal computer. His daddy had said so. Her daddy told everybody they were supposed to be God's servants. Like Jesus was. He didn't even mention presents.

So—no good presents. Rachel had given up on that. But a big role in the primary classes' Christmas play—that shouldn't be too much to ask for. She was by far the best actress in the second grade. *Plus* she went to Sunday school every single week, even when she had the sniffles, or it snowed so hard that she and John and Beth were the only kids there.

"Don't you think a kid who comes every single Sunday no matter if it's a blizzard should get a good part in the primary classes' play?" she asked.

"We live next door to the church, stupid," John had said. "You don't get brownie points for walking across your side yard."

"You're the minister's daughter, Rachel," Beth had said. "It would look bad if you grabbed a big part."

"You got to be Angel Gabriel in both the second *and* third grade," Rachel reminded her.

"That was different," Beth said. "I was the only one in either class who could remember all the lines. The head angel has a lot to say. Besides I speak out. Everyone in the back row heard me perfectly."

"I can speak out," Rachel said, but no one paid any attention.

When she was five, she had been part of the heavenly host. It was a terrible part. The angel costumes were made of a stiff gauzy stuff that itched something awful. Afterward, Mrs. MacLaughlin, who ran the pageant, yelled at her right in front of everybody.

"Rachel Thompson! Angels are spiritual beings! They do not scratch themselves while they sing! You had the congregation laughing at the heavenly host. I was mortified."

Last year Mrs. MacLaughlin had taken a rest from directing, and Ms. Westford had run the pageant. Ms. Westford believed in equal opportunity, so for the first time in the history of First Presbyterian Church, girls had been shepherds and wise men. That was okay with the girls, but the boys were mad. They didn't like the itchy angel costumes at all. And a *lot* of the fathers complained.

But Rachel had been a much better shepherd than those stupid boys. She didn't care what anyone had said afterward. She knew what the Bible meant when it said the shepherds were "sore afraid." When Mr. Nelson shined the spotlight at them to show that the angel of the Lord was about to come upon them, Rachel had shown everyone in the church what it meant to be "sore afraid."

"Help! Help!" she'd cried loud enough to be heard by the people in the very back row. "Don't let it get me!"

The congregation laughed. So did Gabriel and all the shepherds and the entire heavenly host. Mary laughed so hard she started choking, and Joseph had to whack her on the back.

Her father said later that it had been "a brand-new insight on the Christmas story," and her mother said, "Never mind, dear, they weren't laughing at you." But she knew better. No one in the whole church understood what the story was really about. When the Bible said "sore afraid," you were supposed to be scared. When that big light hit her face, Rachel had been trembly all over. She knew in her heart that she was the only kid in the pageant who felt that way. Not even the second- and third-graders who got all the big parts did them right. If you couldn't have a scratching angel, you sure shouldn't have a Joseph yawning so wide you could drive a tractor trailer straight down to his tonsils.

It had been a hard year. Her mother had been tired and pregnant for most of it, and then when David finally was born she'd gotten tired and busy. Beth thought David was the "cutest thing in the world."

"Was I cute when I was little?" Rachel asked her.

"I can't remember," Beth said. "I know you cried a lot. And your face got really red." And she went back to goo-gooing at the baby.

John wasn't as silly, but he was always bragging about how great it was to have a little brother *finally*.

"What's the matter with little sisters?" Rachel asked. John just rolled his eyes.

Now at the end of the worst year of her entire life, Christmas wasn't going to be any better. Even the carols were against her. All those songs about the City of David. "Couldn't we make up a Christmas song about the City of

Rachel?" she asked her mother. But her mother just smiled and kept on singing about David.

"Hey," John said one night, "I just realized. We're all in the Christmas story— David, Elizabeth, John—"

"What about me?" Rachel said. "Oh, you're in it," John said.

"I am?"

"Yeah. I can't remember the verse, but there's something off the side of the story about somebody named Rachel weeping and wailing."

"It's because King Herod killed all her children," Beth said.

It wasn't fair. Everyone else had a nice place in the story—everyone but Rachel. It made her more determined than ever to have a good part in the play, one in which she would not scratch or yell or wail. Mary. She would be Mary. She was old enough this year. She was the best actress in the second grade. Surely, even if she was the minister's daughter, Mrs. MacLaughlin would pick her. She'd be so good in class that Mrs. MacLaughlin would just see that nobody deserved to be Mary more than Rachel did.

Besides, her little brother had already been chosen to be Baby Jesus. She ought to be Mary. Jesus shouldn't have a stranger be his mother. It might scare him. "Now," said Mrs. MacLaughlin at the first practice. "It's a good thing we have a lot of kindergarten to third-graders in this church because we have a lot of parts in this play."

"Mrs. MacLaughlin?" Rachel said.

"What is it, Rachel?" Mrs. MacLaughlin's voice sounded a tiny bit impatient, so Rachel talked fast.

"I know I'm the minister's kid and that when I was little, sometimes—"

"Yes, Rachel—"

"Well, I've studied the part really hard, and since my brother is the Baby Jesus, I thought, well, it would probably mean a lot to *him* if—well, if his big sister could be Mary."

"But we don't have sixth-graders in the play, Rachel. Elizabeth's too old."

"I don't mean Elizabeth, Mrs. MacLaughlin. I mean, well, what's the matter with me?"

There was a burst of laughter in the room. Everyone was laughing at her! Rachel's face went scarlet. "Shut up!" she yelled. "I'm serious. I know the story better than anybody here, and it's my brother!" Everyone laughed harder. Even the little ones who were going to be itchy angels were giggling.

"Rachel—dear—" said Mrs. MacLaughlin after she finally got control of the group. "Of course you know the Christmas story—after all, your father is our minister— but—but Mary is a very difficult role."

"I could do it," Rachel muttered, but she knew it was no use. People weren't supposed to laugh at Mary. And everybody laughed at her—when they paid her any attention at all.

"Carrie," Mrs. MacLaughlin was saying. "How would you like to be our Mary this year?"

Carrie Wilson? She had blue eyes and blond curls all the way down her back and didn't look at all like Mary. And that fake smile. It made Rachel sick to her stomach. Carrie Wilson's Mary would look like a plastic wimp. Mary was the handmaid of the Lord, for heaven's sake, not some department-store dummy.

Rachel could hardly listen as Mrs. MacLaughlin went down the list telling everyone what they were supposed to be. She knew now she wouldn't even get a speaking part. Mrs. MacLaughlin didn't like her. Nobody liked her. Not even God. Finally, Mrs. MacLaughlin stopped.

Rachel looked up. She hadn't heard her name. She didn't want to say anything because maybe her name had been called when she wasn't listening and then Mrs. MacLaughlin would have something else to fuss about. But she couldn't stand it. She raised her hand.

"Yes, Rachel?"

"About my part—"

"Yes, Rachel. This year you have a *very* important part."

"I do?"

"Yes. You will be our understudy."

"Our what?"

"Since you know the story *so* well, you will be prepared to *substitute* in case any of our actors become ill or unable to perform."

"Substitute? You mean I don't have a part of my own?"

"You have *all* the parts—in case—Why suppose, for example, Gabriel should lose her voice? You would step in and be our Gabriel."

Jennifer Rouse, the third-grader who had been chosen to be Gabriel, gave Rachel a dirty look. She had no intention of losing her voice. "Or if"—here Mrs. MacLaughlin smiled sadly at Carrie Wilson—"our Mary were to suddenly have to visit her grandmother in Ohio, you would have to step in and be our Mary."

"My grandmother's coming *here* for Christmas, Mrs. MacLaughlin," Carrie said sweetly. Rachel wasn't stupid. She knew what Mrs. MacLaughlin was doing. She wasn't keeping Rachel from having a big part. She was making sure that Rachel wouldn't have any part at all.

She told her mother that she was never going back to Sunday school again in her whole entire life. "Nonsense, dear," her mother said. And, of course, she went back. Ministers' children have to go to Sunday school. It's the law or something.

And then, a miracle happened. One week before Christmas, Carrie Wilson, who wore the world's prissiest little blue leather boots, slipped on the ice in the mall parking lot and broke both her arms. *Both* her arms. Rachel was overcome with exceeding great joy. God did love her. He did! One arm might count as an accident, but two arms were a miracle. God meant business. No matter how determined Mrs. MacLaughlin was to keep her out of the play, God was going to make sure not only that she got in but that she got the most important part in the whole shebang. She was going to be Mary, the handmaid of the Lord.

Of course, she didn't tell anybody how joyful she was. She was too smart for that. When Mrs. MacLaughlin called her on the phone, Rachel practically cried at the news that she would have to pinch-hit for our poor little Carrie. "I'll do my best, Mrs. MacLaughlin," she said quietly and humbly, just like the real Mary would have.

She went early to the dress rehearsal so Mrs. McLaughlin could try the costume on her. It fit perfectly. Well, it would have fit practically anybody. Those robe things weren't exactly any size, but Rachel took it as a good sign when Mrs. MacLaughlin sighed and admitted that, yes, it did fit.

"Don't you worry, Mrs. MacLaughlin," Rachel said. "I'm the understudy. I know the part perfectly." Which was a little silly since Mary didn't say a word, just looked lovingly into the manger while everyone else sang and carried on. But she wanted Mrs. MacLaughlin to know she wasn't going to do anything to make anybody laugh this year. She would be such a good Mary that Mrs. MacLaughlin would be practically down on her knees begging her to take the part again next year. They'd probably have to extend the play past third grade so that they could keep Rachel in the role of Mary until she was grown up and through college and had babies of her own.

"We have to eat early," she told her mother on Christmas Eve. "Mrs. MacLaughlin wants the cast there an hour before the service."

"Thank goodness," said John. "I don't think I could stand another hour of loud glorias sung off-key."

But Rachel didn't care. She was so happy, the glorias just burst from her. Besides, she had to get them all out before seven o'clock. She couldn't let a stray gloria pass her lips when she was behind that manger. God might understand, but Mrs. MacLaughlin sure wouldn't.

She was all dressed in the sky-blue robe, sitting quietly, looking down into the empty manger. Mrs. MacLaughlin, hoarse from yelling at the heavenly hosts, was giving last minute directions to the wise men when suddenly the back door of the sanctuary opened.

"Why, Mrs. Wilson. Carrie—" Mrs. MacLaughlin said.

Rachel jerked up in alarm. It *was* Carrie, standing in the darkened sanctuary, her fake-fur-trimmed coat hanging off her shoulders, both arms bound to the front of her body.

"She insisted," Mrs. Wilson was saying. "She said, 'The show must go on.' I talked to Dr. Franklin, and he said it would be the best thing in the world for her. She was so distressed about letting everyone down that it was having a negative effect on the healing process."

Two mothers yanked the beautiful blue robe off Rachel

and draped it over Carrie's head. "See. It was meant to be," Mrs. Wilson said. "It totally hides the casts."

Rachel slunk off the platform and slumped down in the first pew. No one noticed. All the adults were oohing and ahing about how brave Carrie was to come and save the play.

"Oh, yes, she's in terrible pain," her mother was saying. "But she couldn't bear to disappoint you all."

No one cared that Rachel was disappointed. Not even God. Of course, God had known all along that Carrie would show up at the last minute and steal back the part. God knew everything, and he had let Rachel sing and rejoice and think for a few days that he was on her side, that he had chosen her, like Mary, to be his handmaid. But it was just a big joke. A big, mean joke. She kicked the red carpet at her feet.

"Off stage, off stage, everyone. Time to line up in your places."

Where did you go when there wasn't any place for you? She looked around.

People were beginning to arrive for the service. She slipped farther down in the pew. She didn't want her family to see her. They'd find out soon enough that God had fired her.

She saw her mother carry David up the far aisle. The baby was sucking happily on his pacifier. He would be a good Jesus. Everyone would say so. Mrs. MacLaughlin was waiting at the door to the hall. She took David and said something to Mom, who cocked her head in a doubtful manner. Was she telling Mom that Rachel wasn't going to be Mary after all? If she did, maybe Mom would come over and take her on her lap and tell her she was sorry. No, Mom didn't even look her way.

The play went well. None of the angels cried or scratched. Gabriel knew all her lines and said them loud enough to be heard almost to the back row. The wise men remembered to carry in their gifts and nobody's crown rolled off. Joseph did not yawn, and Mary gazed sweetly into the manger. It was all perfect. Perfect without her. Rachel felt like weeping and wailing like the Rachel in the Bible.

And then, suddenly, a miracle occurred. Baby Jesus began to cry. Not just cry, *scream*. Yell his little lungs out. Carrie Wilson forgot about being Mary. She turned absolutely white, and her eyes went huge, like she was about to panic. She would have probably got up and run, but with her arms bound under her robe she couldn't move. She looked at Joseph. "Do something!" she whispered. Joseph's face went bright red but he didn't move a muscle.

It was all up to Rachel. She jumped from her pew and dashed up the chancel steps. She was still panting when she got to the manger. Rachel poked around under the baby until she located the pacifier and jammed it into David's open mouth. He clamped down on it at once. The big church went silent except for his noisy sucking. Rachel smiled down at him. He was a lovely Jesus.

"Who do you think you are?" Carrie Wilson hissed through her teeth. But the whisper was almost loud enough to be heard in the back row. Rachel could hear a snicker from somewhere out in the darkened sanctuary.

"Behold." Rachel straightened up and stared sternly in the direction of the offender. There was no doubt that the people in the last pew could hear her. "I am the handmaid of the Lord! And I say unto you, glory to God in the highest and on earth peace and goodwill to men, women, and children."

Nobody laughed. They didn't dare.

A Stubborn Sweetness

The call came early Christmas Eve morning. I was still asleep, and my voice must have sounded peevish when I answered the phone.

"You needn't be annoyed with me, Judson," my sister said. "I can't help it."

"What is it, Fran?"

"What do you think it is? Why else would I call you at this hour?"

"Father?"

"Of course it's Father," she said. "The doctor is sure he won't last another day. He thinks you should come immediately."

Part of me wanted to protest. I didn't want to leave my wife and children at Christmastime. What did it matter if I came or not? My father had not recognized me for ages.

I dutifully went to see him three or four times a year. He would sit in his chair in the sterile nursing home, nodding at me. Sometimes, when he was most alert, he would call me Wesley. Wesley was my brother, who died in Vietnam.

But usually he would mumble things I could not understand and nod uncomprehendingly as I would vainly try to carry on a conversation.

Once he looked me straight in the face, his eyes clearing, so that I thought for a moment he knew me, and perhaps he did, for what he said was: "Tell your mother Wesley's home." This time I nodded stupidly, not even trying to remind him that both Mother and Wesley had been dead for many years.

Part of me did not want to go and say good-bye to an old man who could not hear me, who had hardly listened to me even when we were both younger. And yet, I had to go. My wife understood, even though the children did not. "You need to go, Judson," Marilyn said, "not just for Fran's sake—for your own."

I drove myself to the airport, bought a standby ticket, and watched three flights take off without me. Each time, I called Fran to ask how he was. "You've got to hurry!" she'd say. But it was late afternoon before I got a plane headed for Springfield. When we landed, I called Marilyn. But when I tried to reach Fran, the line was busy, so rather than waste time, I rented a car and started the fifty-mile drive. The road on which I was traveling was new, but the countryside was the farmland in which I had grown up. The sky on this Christmas Eve was clear and star-filled, spreading peace over the rolling hills and the shadow of the mountain beyond. The world of regrets and sorrow and imminent death seemed far away.

I thought about my father—not the invalid he had become, but as I had known him when I was a boy. He was a strong, gruff man, a farmer who owed no man anything. If Wesley had lived, I think I might have grown up without my father ever really noticing me. Perhaps I'm unjust. I'm sure my mother would say so. She was forever trying to interpret us to each other, and for her sake, as we both grew older, we tried to understand. It was she on that terrible Christmas after Wesley's death . . .

Just then, my headlights caught a figure stepping out into the road. I swerved and missed, but I was shaken and, as I straightened the car, my heart still pounding, I caught a glimpse in the rearview mirror of the person I had nearly struck. He was in the road, waving his arms at me.

Without thinking, I stopped the car and began to back slowly down the shoulder. When I got alongside, I stuck my head out the window and shouted, "Get off the road! I nearly hit you!" It wasn't a man. It was a young girl, her hair streaming across a rucksack on her back. She wore no hat or gloves.

"Yeah?" Her chin was up. "Watch where you're going." Then suddenly, almost coy, "Hey, gimme a ride to town?" Without waiting for me to answer, she reached behind me, unlatched the back door, and was in the car before I could protest.

As I shifted into drive and moved out into the road, she swung the pack off her back and put it on the seat beside her. I had seen enough of her face now to realize that she was about the age of my daughter Jennie, who was barely fourteen.

"Where are you headed?" I asked, trying to sound casual.

"Who needs to know?"

"No one. I couldn't help wondering. You remind me of my daughter."

"Well, I ain't. Lucky you."

We drove on in silence. She was wrestling something from her rucksack. I switched on the radio. My car was filled with the joyful sound of a carol. My mind went from the waif behind me to my mother. She had loved Christmas so, especially the music. It was then that I felt the hard, round pressure against my right shoulder.

"Shut that thing off," she ordered.

I turned off the radio, too amazed to be truly frightened. Where on earth had the child gotten a gun?

"Now pass me back your wallet and watch. Anything valuable."

"I'll have to stop the car first."

"Okay, but no fooling around, hear?"

I eased the car onto the shoulder and shut off the engine. She held the gun, pointing roughly at my right ear while I got out of the car, took off my watch and wedding ring, and unloaded the pockets of my overcoat and trousers. I put the contents onto the passenger seat. Her hand was shaking as the gun followed my every move. I wasn't afraid she would shoot deliberately, but in her anxiety, she might accidently—and then as I straightened up to close the door, I looked more closely at the trembling weapon. The car's dim overhead light gave away its secret. The gun was a toy.

My impulse was to grab it, laughing, but the look on her face stopped me.

Instead, I shut the door and began walking down the road.

She yelled after me. "Where the hell you think you're going?"

"I thought you wanted the car as well."

"Come back here," she said, her voice breaking. "I can't drive."

I came back and got in. The gun was at my shoulder at once. "Now go," she said, "and don't try to make a fool outta me again." She wasn't crying, but she was close to it.

"Don't use the credit cards."

"Shut up and drive."

"Seriously, they'll get you right away. There's about two hundred in cash, and day after tomorrow, you should be able to pawn the watch for at least a hundred. It's antique gold."

"What's with you?"

"I'm trying to help. I ran away from home once. It's no fun."

"I don't need help."

"Well, you do need money. You can't get far without that."

"Don't I know," she mumbled. After a minute, she poked me hard with the plastic gun barrel. "You on the level about the credit cards?" she asked.

"I swear they're not worth it. I'd have to report them stolen."

"What about the watch and stuff?"

"If you'll let me have my wedding ring and the credit cards, you can take the money and the watch, and I'll consider them a Christmas present."

"Meaning?"

"I won't even call the police."

"Mister Santa Claus himself." Her voice was sarcastic, but the pressure on my shoulder lessened for a moment, and then she jabbed me hard. "You putting me on. I could kill you, you know."

"But it wouldn't be smart," I said. "And you don't strike me as a dumb person."

She snorted. "That isn't what my dad said. And he should know."

"Fathers aren't always right. My father . . ."

"Forget your father."

"I can't forget my father," I said. "He's dying. That's where I'm going. To see him once more before he dies."

"Dying?"

"It's all right. He's very old and sick. He's ready to die."

"Ask him. You might get another opinion."

"You think so?"

"I don't want to talk about it."

"Well, you're young. . ."

"But I might die," she blurted out. "Oh, God, I might die." The gun fell from my shoulder to the floor as she put both her hands to her face and began to cry.

"You dropped your gun," I said quietly. She stopped crying instantly, snatched up the gun, poked me three or four times, then dropped it again. "You knew it was fake all the time, didn't you?"

I nodded.

"My dad is right. I'm the dumbest bitch in the world."

"You're not so dumb."

"Yeah? Then how come I'm pregnant?" She was almost yelling.

"Is that why you ran away?"

"It was either that or get throwed out. He don't care if I live or die. Long as I don't bother him."

My first thought was to rush in with words of reassurance. Of course her father cared. Even now he must be calling the state police, asking them to help him find her. But I kept quiet. I knew I was thinking of my father—what he would have done. I didn't know this child's father. And suddenly, I wanted to give her my father—for all his sternness and anger and doubts—because I knew what my father would have done.

"May I tell you a story?"

For an answer, she blew her nose loudly.

"It was in 1967," I began, realizing that the Christmas of 1967 was as remote to her as the first Christmas. "In early November we had word through the Red Cross that my brother Wesley was dead. His plane had crashed over North Vietnam two years before. He—he died in prison." For a minute the cold pain of Wesley's death returned. I had adored him.

"So?" she prompted, impatient to be done.

"It wasn't only that he was dead, but the way he died that hurt my father so. I think if he had been killed in the crash, my father would have been able to bear it. But it was the waste, the agony of his dying bit by bit in prison—"

"You do a lot of talk about dying," she said.

"Sorry. I'm trying to figure out why my father was so terribly bitter. He had always been a very religious man. He even named his sons after church heroes, but once he heard the news about Wesley, he stopped going to church, stopped saying grace at meals. He even tried to keep my mother from taking me and my sister to Sunday school. I was only nine. I couldn't understand."

"Easy," she said. "Sometimes you gotta pay God back."

"Well, Christmas came, and I was supposed to sing a solo in the Sunday school program. I was all excited about it, and so was my mother. I could tell that even my sister, who usually ignored me, was proud that I had been chosen.

The night of the program my mother tried to persuade my father to go. I was a bit afraid of my father. I was worried that if he went he might be disappointed in me, so I wasn't sure I wanted him to go, but I wanted my mother to be happy. That was the real reason I wanted him to go."

"You should've left him alone."

"Yes, we should have, I guess. Anyhow, at suppertime my mother said that he owed it to me to go, that it was a big night in my life, and he would be proud to hear how well I sang. 'He can sing it right here in the kitchen for me,' my father said."

"You should've done it."

"I did. I stood there in the kitchen after supper while he drank his coffee, and I sang for him. Do you know 'There's a Song in the Air'?"

"I don't know classical. I don't like it either."

"Don't worry. I won't sing it for you," I said. "But I sang it for him, and the more I sang, the more frightened I became. I could tell he was about to burst with rage. Even before I finished, he slammed his fist on the table and sloshed coffee all over the cloth. 'Lies!' he yelled. 'It's all lies!' Then he jumped up and grabbed me by the shoulders. He was like a crazy man. 'Don't you know what the world is like, Judson? There's no pretty angels flapping their wings. There's no singing in the sky. There's hate and suffering and cruel, cruel death!' Then he shoved me aside and grabbed my mother. 'I don't see it, Agnes. How you can hang onto all this nonsense! The air's not full of music. It's full of bombs crashing and people screaming!'

"My mother's face tightened, and she said very quietly, 'The song is louder.'"

"My father began to curse. I had never heard him speak

a word to my mother in anger, and now, all because of me, because I wanted to sing in the stupid Sunday school program, he was cursing her. I ran out of the house. It was a cold night, but it was a long time before I slowed down enough to notice. I was never going back. He had always despised me, I told myself. It was only for Wesley's sake that he had put up with me. Now Wesley was gone, so I was going, too. Before I knew it, I was deep in the woods, almost at the foot of that mountain over there, just as lost as I could be, and it was bitter cold."

"I take it you didn't freeze to death," she said sarcastically.

"No. I kept walking, but it was a perfectly black night with no moon. I couldn't even see a tree before I bumped into it. I was terrified—all that trackless night. I was sure I was going to die out there in the cold dark all alone."

"Yeah," she said without a trace of sarcasm.

"And then, suddenly, I saw a light way off in the distance. I began to stumble toward it. It was the most wonderful thing I'd ever seen in my life, that light. I still couldn't see where I was walking, but it didn't matter. I just kept my eyes on the light."

"And you run smack into an angel of God Almighty."

"No. It was my father. He had come out to look for me."

"So he falls down on his knees and begs you to forgive him and you live happy ever after."

"No. I just went home with him. It was too late by then for any of us to go to the program. So that was that. We never spoke about it again."

"You can let me out here," she said. I hadn't realized that we were already at the edge of town.

"I don't like to just drop you off this time of night."

"No problem."

"Look. We're almost at the nursing home. Why don't you wait? As soon as I've seen my father, I'll take you home."

She made a sound, meant to be a laugh. "Don't do me any favors, mister."

I pulled up in front of the home. When I'd parked, I put on my wedding ring, took the money out of my wallet, and laid it on the front seat.

"I don't want your watch," she said. "You can take it."

"Thanks," I said. "Why don't you wait? I won't be but a minute, and then—"

She jerked her head in a nod.

"You're too late," Fran said. "He's not responding to anyone now."

I went to the bedside and took my father's big hand. It was thinner than I'd remembered. He looked peaceful.

"He recognized me this afternoon," Fran said. "He spoke to me."

"Did he?" I was remembering the light, how he had come for me that night through the darkness.

"It didn't make much sense," she continued. "His voice was stronger than it's been for years. He said—'Tell your mother the song is louder.'"

"I'll be right back," I said, almost running out. The car was empty. As I opened the front door to be sure, the light revealed a twenty-dollar bill on the seat. She hadn't wanted to leave me penniless.

I never saw her again. I could not tell her my father's last words. Not that she would have understood. But then, in a way, he was wrong. Both he and my mother were wrong.

The song is not louder. It is swallowed up quickly in the cry of anger or the clack of greed. No, the song is not louder, but it persists. It comes, as it had come to me beside my father's bed, a melody of the most stubborn sweetness, for which we are never prepared. And we turn away from it again and again and again.

"But oh, my child," I said to the empty night, "even though the song is not louder, it is stronger. And someday it will find you—out there alone in the darkness."

Then I turned and went back in to say good-bye to my father.